The Letters of Louise Ritter From 1893 to 1925

A Swiss-German Immigrant Woman To Antelope County, Nebraska

Dr. & Mrs. Luenenghoener -
Two people who have been and
continue to be important to
all Midlanders.

Darlene M. Ritter

Darlene Ritter

Siegenthaler-Ritter, Publishers
Fremont, Nebraska

ISBN 0-9609372-0-X
Library of Congress Catalog Card Number:
82-607-61

Printed in the United States of America
by
Service Press
Henderson, Nebraska 68371

Louise Siegenthaler-Ritter

Looking directly into life
With unfaltering faith –
Faith that "God will do it right."
Swiss Alps replaced by
Nebraska prairies,
Distances dividing love.
Sisters, Brother,
Father, Mother – Swiss;
Husband, Sons – American;
She – a part of each.

With letters trying to bind them
Letters filled with "I wish,
I hope, I miss."
Loneliness mixed with triumph.

Remembered
Wife, Mother, Grandmother.

TABLE OF CONTENTS

PREFACE   xi

INTRODUCTION   1

NOTES ON MANUSCRIPT AND EDITING   17

MAPS OF SWITZERLAND   18-19

MAPS OF NEBRASKA
 AND ANTELOPE COUNTY   20

INTRODUCTORY NOTE FOR LETTER OF
 AUGUST 27, 1893   21
  Letter of August 27, 1893 24

INTRODUCTORY NOTE FOR LETTERS OF
 OCTOBER 22 AND CHRISTMAS, 1893   29
  Letter of October 22, 1893   29
  Letter of Christmas 1893   31

INTRODUCTORY NOTE FOR LETTERS OF
 JANUARY 28 AND FEBRUARY 8, 1894   35
  Letter of January 28, 1894   35
  Letter of February 8, 1894   36

INTRODUCTORY NOTE FOR LETTER OF
 NOVEMBER 19, 1894   39
  Letter of November 19, 1894   39

SUMMARY OF 1895   43

INTRODUCTORY NOTE FOR LETTER OF
 OCTOBER 25, 1896   45
  Letter of October 25, 1896   45

INTRODUCTORY NOTE FOR LETTER OF
 APRIL 15, 1897   49
  Letter of April 15, 1897   49

INTRODUCTORY NOTE FOR LETTERS OF SEPTEMBER 4,
    DECEMBER 11, 1898 AND FEBRUARY 26, 1899   53
      Letter of September 4, 1898   53
      Letter of December 11, 1898   54
      Letter of February 26, 1899   55

INTRODUCTORY NOTE FOR LETTER OF
    JULY 8, 1900   59
      Letter of July 8, 1900   60

INTRODUCTORY NOTE FOR LETTER OF
    JANUARY 1902   63
      Letter of January 1902   63

INTRODUCTORY NOTE FOR LETTERS OF JUNE 1
    AND JUNE 20, 1902   65
      Letter of June 1, 1902   65
      Letter of June 20, 1902   66

INTRODUCTORY NOTE FOR LETTERS OF SEPTEMBER 8,
    DECEMBER 27, 1903, AND JANUARY 24, 1904   69
      Letter of September 8, 1903   71
      Letter of December 27, 1903   72
      Letter of January 24, 1904   73

INTRODUCTORY NOTE FOR LETTERS OF SEPTEMBER 18, 1904,
    AND JANUARY 8, 1905   77
      Letter of September 18, 1904   78
      Letter of January 8, 1905   79

INTRODUCTORY NOTE FOR LETTERS OF
    MARCH 5 AND 26, 1905   81
      Letter of March 5, 1905   82
      Letter of March 26, 1905   82

INTRODUCTORY NOTE FOR LETTERS OF JULY 4, JULY 19,
    OCTOBER 8, 1905, AND JANUARY 21, 1906   85
      Letter of July 4, 1905   85
      Letter of July 19, 1905   86
      Letter of October 8, 1905   87
      Letter of January 21, 1906   88

INTRODUCTORY NOTE FOR LETTERS OF JULY 30,
   AUGUST 19, AND DECEMBER 20, 1906 91
      Letter of July 30, 1906 91
      Letter of August 19, 1906 93
      Letter of December 20, 1906 94

INTRODUCTORY NOTE FOR LETTERS OF
   FEBRUARY 24 AND JULY 28, 1907 97
      Letter of February 24, 1907 97
      Letter of July 28, 1907 98

INTRODUCTORY NOTE FOR TWO LETTERS OF
   DECEMBER 21, 1907 101
      Letter of December 21, 1907 to Her Mother 101
      Letter of December 21, 1907 to Her Sister 102

INTRODUCTORY NOTE FOR LETTER OF
   JUNE 11, 1908 105
      Letter of June 11, 1908 105

INTRODUCTORY NOTE FOR LETTER OF
   DECEMBER 26, 1908 109
      Letter of December 26, 1908 109

INTRODUCTORY NOTE FOR LETTER OF
   MARCH 21, 1909 111
      Letter of March 21, 1909 111

INTRODUCTORY NOTE FOR LETTER OF
   MAY 14, 1910 113
      Letter of May 14, 1910 113

INTRODUCTORY NOTE FOR LETTERS OF
   DECEMBER 24, 1911, AND JANUARY 1, 1912 115
      Letter of December 24, 1911 115
      Letter of January 1, 1912 116

INTRODUCTORY NOTE FOR LETTERS OF
   MAY 10 AND AUGUST, 1912 119
      Letter of May 10, 1912 119
      Letter of August, 1912 120

INTRODUCTORY NOTE FOR LETTERS OF
   JANUARY 1 AND 5, 1913 123
     Letter of January 1, 1913 123
     Letter of January 5, 1913 124

INTRODUCTORY NOTE FOR LETTERS OF JUNE 18
   AND DECEMBER 17, 1913 127
     Letter of June 18, 1913 127
     Letter of December 17, 1913 128

INTRODUCTORY NOTE FOR LETTERS OF
   APRIL 2 AND NOVEMBER 21, 1915 131
     Letter of April 2, 1915 132
     Letter of November 21, 1915 133

SUMMARY OF THE YEARS 1916, 1917, AND 1918 135

INTRODUCTORY NOTE FOR LETTER OF
   DECEMBER 30, 1919 139
     Letter of December 30, 1919 139

INTRODUCTORY NOTE FOR LETTERS OF
   JUNE 8, DECEMBER 6 AND 7, 1920 141
     Letter of June 8, 1920 142
     Letter of December 6, 1920 143
     Letter of December 7, 1920 144

INTRODUCTORY NOTE FOR LETTERS OF JUNE 27 AND
   DECEMBER 28, 1921, AND FEBRUARY 9, 1922 147
     Letter of June 27, 1921 147
     Letter of December 28, 1921 148
     Letter of February 9, 1922 150

INTRODUCTORY NOTE FOR LETTER OF
   JANUARY 1923 153
     Letter of January 1923 153

INTRODUCTORY NOTE FOR LETTER OF
   DECEMBER 16, 1923 155
     Letter of December 16, 1923 155

INTRODUCTORY NOTE FOR LETTER OF
   AUGUST 1924 157
      Letter of August 1924 158

INTRODUCTORY NOTE FOR LETTER OF
   JANUARY 13, 1925 161
      Letter of January 13, 1925 162

AFTERWORD 165

OBITUARY 167

APPENDIX I... 169

APPENDIX II 170

APPENDIX III 171

BIBLIOGRAPHY 173

PREFACE

Fred Ritter, my grandfather, was a Swiss immigrant who came with his wife and sons to Antelope County, Nebraska, to improve the family economic situation. I grew up listening to his stories about the early hard times in Nebraska and about Switzerland or the Old Country. William Tell was as familiar a character to me as Cinderella. He said little about his wife who died in 1925, leaving him a widower for thirty-four years; but in his room he had a large picture of her, and when he spoke of her it was with emotion. He told me once that since she had not been able to return to Switzerland to visit, it would not be right for him to ever return.

Six years after his death, I traveled to Europe and visited Iffwyl, Switzerland, to see where my grandparents lived before they immigrated. During my short visit, I met many relatives and learned for the first time that after my grandmother's death there had been no communication between the families until the letter telling them I would arrive for a visit. I also learned that Louise Ritter-Siegenthaler, their aunt and my grandmother, had maintained a correspondence with her family in Switzerland from the time of their immigration in 1893 until her death in 1925. During those years, letters written to her parents, her sister Anna, and others were saved. They were in Anna's possession until her death in 1951. Then the letters were kept by her youngest daughter, Klara. It was in her home that I was shown the letters and learned of their existence and of their importance to the Swiss branch of the family. Since that time, the families have visited and corresponded with each other.

In 1972, Klara Wuthrich-Stucki gave me most of the letters. She said that they now meant more to me than they would to anyone of the next generation in Switzerland. I am grateful that they treasured them for so long and chose to share them with me.

Since the time I received the letters, I have wanted to edit them. They provided a link to the grandmother I never knew. Editing them and making them available to other readers is a way for me to affirm her role in the saga of American immigration and to pay tribute to the pioneer grandfather I knew and loved.

The letters were written in Old German script, and I am indebted to Maria Rosenblatt, Professor Emeritus of Midland Lutheran College, for her translation of the script, thus enabling me to know my grandmother. An expression of gratitude is due my parents, Mr. and Mrs. Ernest Ritter, for their willingness to go through family records and their personal memories to help me understand some of the references in the letters. I am grateful to Dr. Bernice Slote, who sparked my interest in Plains literature and thus inspired me to pursue a project of this type. A special word of appreciation is due Dr. Paul Olson, whose counsel and encouragement have enabled me to complete this project.

INTRODUCTION

On March 22, 1893, Louise Ritter-Siegenthaler at age thirty began her journey to Nebraska from Iffwyl, Canton Bern, Switzerland. She was accompanied by her husband, Fritz, and three sons, ages six, four and three months. She left behind her in Switzerland her parents, two sisters, and a brother – a close family unit – and the beauty of the Bernese Oberland. The family traveled from Bern via Le Havre to Southampton where they boarded the *City of Paris* on March 25 and traveled second class to New York City, arriving April 9, 1893. After a brief stop in New York, they boarded a train and traveled to Tilden, Nebraska.[1] Fritz's unmarried older brother, Jakob, had come a year earlier and had made arrangements for them by buying a quarter section of land which included a fully furnished house.[2] After her arrival, Louise began a correspondence with her family which continued until her death in 1925. Her story is one of many of this period of our national history – a part of the larger saga of the American immigration movement.

Louise Ritter-Siegenthaler's letters are treated as part of a larger middle European immigration to the Great Plains, documents valuable both for literary and for historical and sociological studies. The population of the United States today, except for the Indians, consists of immigrants and descendants of immigrants. Of the seventy million or so people who have migrated from Europe since 1600, about two-thirds came to America.[3] Not only did the United States receive a greater number of immigrants than any other country in the world, but it also received the greatest variety of people. After freely admitting millions of people from these foreign countries, Americans began to speculate on the effect of this large number of aliens on national unity. World War I, which came approximately twenty-five years after Louise emigrated, brought this question to the foreground. After the war, the feeling was that unchecked immigration could lead only to a loss of national solidarity for the United States.[4] Because of public pressure, Congress in 1921 passed an act placing a preliminary control on immigration which set quotas – three percent of the number of foreign born persons of that nationality resident in the United States at the time of the 1910 census. In 1924 the Johnson-Reed Act was passed. This laid down a permanent basis for admission to the United States. It placed a limit of 150,000 immigrants in any one year and assigned quotas to each nationality in proportion to its contribution to the existing American population.[5] The enactment of this law closed a momentous chapter in American and European history. It also closed a door on close cultural ties between the immigrants and the old country and reinforced the movement to prevent them from using their native languages.

There have been and continue to be studies of immigration to the United States – sociological, historical, psychological, economic. The great immigration has provided subject matter for art. The studies sometimes begin with the colonization of the Atlantic States, or they specialize on a particular region; others concentrate on the immigration which settled the Midwest and Plains states. The addition to the population of the United State between 1815 and 1914 of thirty-five million Europeans is as significant a chapter in American history as the preceding two centuries of colonization.[6] Everyone is familiar with the stages of settlement of the West. First came the mountain men, the hunters and trappers. Following them came the more permanent settlers. Because the European newcomer was not, in the American sense, a frontiersman, but had an aversion to the wilderness with its solitude, loneliness, and primitive mode of life, he followed the frontiersman and the pioneer farmers.[7] By the 1870s the Middle European immigrant had reached the prairies. While the immigrants were moving in, many of the Americans were moving out. This gave the invaders a beginning which they expanded quietly and steadily during the following decades.[8] They came for many reasons – pressure of population, religious zeal and persecution, economic motives, love of adventure, and political ambition.[9]

Whatever their reasons, they came by the millions. Statistics for a few decades give some indication of the numbers of these immigrants. From 1861 to 1870, 2,598,214 arrived; 1871-1880, 2,314,824; 1881-1890, 5,246,-613; 1891-1900, 3,687,564; and from 1901-1910, 8,795,386.[10] The small country of Switzerland had 297,835 persons emigrate to the United States from 1820 to 1945.[11] At first the newspapers in the countries of departure commented on the sight of trains of wagons loaded with household gear and children which were followed by men and women on foot traveling from the interior to the port of embarkation. On the other side of the ocean American papers reported the arrival of these groups, but after a short time these events became too common to record.[12] These people came from many parts of Europe and later from other parts of the world to locate in a new and unknown land.

The arrival of these millions altered America, but it must be remembered that immigration also altered the immigrants. Immigration resulted in one's becoming a foreigner, ceasing to belong. The disruption of a familiar life and surroundings often caused broken homes, and the effect of the movement was harder upon the people than upon the society they entered.[13] Later generations forgot that emigration uprooted these people from their traditional environment with its known behavior patterns and replanted them in a strange setting, among strangers, where strange manners prevailed. Old behavior patterns were no longer adequate because the problems of life were new and different. They were forced to work out new ways for determining the meaning of their lives, often under harsh and hostile circumstances.[14] It is too easy to dwell only on the promise of the new land and ignore the cost. Once old ties are snapped where and how does one define his significance as an individual? The alienation experienced by the sensitive and lost father of Antonia Shimerda in Cather's famous novel *My Antonia* was too much; he took his own life. Louise never experienced the suicidal despair of Shimerda, but her letters are a record of the anguish of separation.

It is much easier to live if some actions are decided or some decisions are made because of the milieu in which one lives – if social behavior is largely habitual. Because the immigrants no longer had the institutions and social patterns which formerly guided their actions, they often lived in crisis; and it took time to establish new patterns adapted to their new location. This shock, and the effects of the shock, lasted many years, influencing generations which themselves never paid the cost of crossing.[15] If this is true, it is reason enough for not forgetting the immigrant experience and making an attempt to understand it. In understanding those who were transplanted, we can perhaps better understand ourselves.

Certainly, there have been many who have felt the need for studying immigration. At first the social scientists were concerned with immigration problems. They emphasized the rapid settlement and the Americanization of the immigrants. In addition, many enthusiastic individuals concentrated on their own ancestry. The amount of information on such ethnic groups as the Scandinavians, Czechs, Bohemians, and Russian-Germans gives evidence of this interest. Both the early social scientists and the early cultural nationalists tended to concentrate on the successful individuals who gained fame and prominence. During the last thirty years, the study of immigration has broadened into historical, sociological, and psychological studies. This has altered the emphasis of the earlier studies. The change in emphasis had led to a greater concentration on the financial and psychological price paid by immigrants. Theodore Blegen explained the change as follows: "We have pushed behind the barricade of statistics to learn the American immigrant was not a problem, but a human being."[16]

Before these changes, only novelists seemed to remember that immigrants were people too, and that immigration involved them and their societies as well as America.[17] Ole Rölvaag in *Giants in the Earth* records the effect of the disruption on the family, especially on the wife and mother, Beret Holm. Other works such as Mari Sandoz's *Old Jules* or Sophus Winter's *Take All to Nebraska* include only slightly, if at all, fictionalized accounts of the heavy human costs. So while the immigrants had an effect on America, it is well to keep in mind that the effect on the individual immigrant could be as recorded in a Swedish volume: "I have been successful. I have property. My children have superior advantages. But *I have lost my life.*"[18] It may be too much to say that in emigration, Louise had "lost her life," but her isolation as recorded in her letters, particularly in later life, was certainly deep.

3

The letters that people have written home describing a new situation or location have always been invaluable sources for individual attitudes. Studies of letters have helped provide a valuable corrective to the information secured by those taking the so-called objective approaches to the great immigration. The private letter has a long history, but for most of the farmers and workmen of European countries it was a novelty. In the wake of emigration it became a means of communication for the common people. The first letter from America was a rarity, a strange event which caused a stir far beyond the recipient's immediate circle. Later, as emigration increased, more and more letters arrived. The sensation caused by the first letters might have decreased, but a letter from America was never looked upon as a common, everyday event. We know that the letter from the American emigrant was opened with great excitement, perused with interest, read by many people, and discussed; that at least, was the case with Louise's letters. Often the letter was copied and sent on to others, and some of the letters were even published in newspapers.[19] In his book *Land of Their Choice,* Theodore Blegen has presented a collection of letters written by Norwegian immigrants to their homeland. He speaks of these letters as "a little-known human story that is a part of the larger saga of America."[20]

One of the "little known human stories" is told through the collected letters of the Swiss immigrant woman, Louise Siegenthaler-Ritter, who wrote from Nebraska to her relatives in Switzerland. Louise's letters reflect a woman's reaction to her pioneering experience in Tilden, Nebraska, during the years 1893 to 1925, from her arrival in Nebraska to her death. They also represent a group about whom little study has been done – the German-Swiss. The history of the letters supports some of the generalizations already given. They were collected by the sister of Louise Ritter and were kept by the youngest daughter after her mother died. The letters had been read and reread by at least nine family members, and they were circulated among family members from Lausanne through villages around Bern to Zurich before they were given to the granddaughter of their author.

The letters written by millions of immigrants also served to draw two continents together. Ties were developed between American towns or counties and secluded European villages. The first person to set forth from one of these villages was remembered by family and neighbors. In later years, he was still remembered by old residents as a sort of legendary character. The first member of a family to venture on the journey long continued to be the principal topic of conversation. The last words at the parting undoubtedly were to "write soon."[21] Of course, as the numbers of those leaving their homelands increased so did the number of letters. These letters contained advice from one human being to another and often encouraged another family member to come to the United States. In a household which received these letters from America, the far country ceased to be a vague geographi-

4

cal designation. For example, the letters which follow linked a small town in Nebraska – Tilden – to the Swiss villages of Ins, Iffwyl, and others.[22] Louise was not successful in persuading any member of her family to come to Nebraska during her lifetime, but her husband's brother and three of his sisters did settle in the same area. Her husband was himself one of those who followed the guidance and directions of his brother, Jakob, who had come over earlier and had written back to the family.

Louise Ritter's letters are, first of all, those of an immigrant woman. Letters back to Europe were written by both men and women who recorded different responses to their experiences in the new land. Generalizations frequently indicate that the men were happy with the challenge of the Plains, but women were repelled by them. "There was too much of the unknown, too few of the things they loved."[23] Beret Holm's response to the Plains was that there was nothing to hide behind. It was too open. The loneliness which women endured on the Great Plains could crush the soul if they could not meet the isolation with an adventurous spirit.[24] There were some women presented in literature like Alexandra Bergson in Willa Cather's *O Pioneers!* who had the spirit which kept them from being crushed. This fictional woman had triumphed, but she had not come as a wife and mother. She did not face the problems of a Beret Holm on how to provide a civilized life for her children. But even Alexandra admitted that the life of a pioneer had cost her. "Maybe I would never have been very soft, anyhow; but I certainly didn't choose to be the kind of girl I was. If you take even a vine and cut it back again and again, it grows hard, like a tree."[25] Many of the vines cut back did not grow again.

There can be no doubt that in many instances the life of the farm woman was intolerable, unutterably lonely. Fiction often shows the Plains having an appalling effect on women. Certainly, the wind, the sand, the drought, the sun, and the boundless expanse of a horizon on which appeared mirages seemed to overwhelm some women with a sense of desolation and futility.[26] But this is not the whole story in either fiction or real life. Many immigrant wives had much less work to do than their counterparts back home because they had been set free from field and barn work. The rising status of many families was marked not only by a bigger house and better farm machinery, but by such conveniences as water in the house, a washing machine pumped by hand, and gas lights. Louise Ritter might have been unhappy because she was separated from her family and felt the loss of a cultural context, but she proudly told her family about the conveniences that she and her husband were able to acquire to help them in their work.

It is never safe to generalize on the unhappiness, fear, or other emotions of the millions of women who immigrated – sometimes with their families and sometimes by themselves. Many of them are known only through fragments of their lives on the Plains. They traveled westward in everything from covered wagons to river boats, in jolting railway cars; and some of them even walked, pushing handcarts before them. Certainly, many women were willing to accompany their men because of the desire for an easier and more plentiful living. For others there was "the lure of the unknown, and an intense spirit which historians usually describe as 'manifest destiny'."[27] According to Oscar Handlin, the reason that we know so little about the millions of families drawn from the humblest levels of society is that historians devoted most of their attention to exceptional individuals who distinguished themselves by success in the New World.[28] The content of the letters and diaries of some of the humble millions supports the Swede who acknowledged he had gained financial security, but had lost his life.

With painful effort and at the sacrifice of precious time, letters were written to express the solidarity the immigrants still felt with those who stayed behind. The letter was the symbol of the ties that continued to bind them together.[29] The letters of Louise Ritter record thirty-two years of solidarity with those who stayed behind. The expression of solidarity comes through salutations: to my dears, to my aunt, sister, uncle, cousin, friend, to every person who filled the days of the old life and will never be seen again. The letters of immigrants were often directed to the aging parents who bore and cared, who took trouble over, shed tears for them, and now were left alone. With the greeting went wishes that those back in the beloved homeland might have years of life, of health and happiness, which were elusive both there and here.[30] These greetings and salutations have been included with the letters of Louise Ritter because in their repetition they illustrate these wishes – at least in her individual history.

Every time one is tempted to dwell on the loneliness and backward look of the immigrants, a reminder of their lives in the new land appears. Life meant more than a living, more than sheer survival. The immigrants were people who fell in love, married, and had children. They faced the business of learning a new language. They became involved in the politics and government and helped elect officials. They made friends and gained neighbors and became participants of communities. They were concerned about schools for their children. Many found in this land the opportunity for the better days they dreamed of for so many years.[31] This is almost an outline of much of the subject matter found in the letters of Louise Ritter. The title of Dorothy Skårdal's book *The Divided Heart* states the dilemma of the immigrant. She was of both worlds. Skårdal's book, which deals with Scandinavians, aptly characterizes the loyalties of this Swiss immigrant as well as of the Scandinavians. Skårdal speaks of the rings of loyalty which moved out from the family center, the main basis of solidarity in the homeland. The importance of kinship naturally continued in the New World since it was one constant element where all else was different. Therefore, if an immigrant had any relative in America and knew where he might be found, the newcomer would often head straight for the relative when he or she got off the boat.[32] The next loyalty Skårdal identifies is that of acquaintanceship. Even if two people had not known each other well before, that older shared experience drew them together when both became strangers in their new environment. The third loyalty was for those who shared a home country or province or dialect. Later arrivals from the same valley renewed for earlier immigrants the bond of their own past. Therefore time and again in pioneer days, newcomers were welcomed by settlers who had come from the same region, and the older people came from miles around to hear the latest news of those and the area they had left so many years before.[33] All of these loyalties are present in Louise Ritter's letters.

Because of the strong theme of homesickness throughout Louise's letters, it is appropriate to note Skårdal's explanation for the Scandinavian homesickness. Some remained homesick regardless of prosperity. Often these were persons too rigid to adapt to new conditions. They might have been too old and fixed in their ways at the time of emigration, or too emotionally bound to family friends to be able to develop new emotional ties in a strange land.[34] A Swiss immigrant blamed his loneliness on the fact that citizens of mountainous countries, "and especially of the beautiful Switzerland, when they go to foreign countries for a lengthy period, are visited with a peculiar mind and soul affliction known as **home**sickness." He continues by stating he experienced this more than once and most forcefully in the beginning of the year 1913, after thirty-three years of travel in different parts of the United States. He cured his homesickness by a return visit to his homeland.[35] A return trip was not possible until too late for Louise Ritter; early after the emigration, she had to live with her homesickness. Later, she was too old and the ties were too extended for a return.

It would be impossible in any single work to incorporate or even summarize all that has been done in recording many of the groups who came to the United States and especially to the Great Plains. There is still work to be done with some groups. Many articles and some brief volumes have been written about emigration from Denmark, Finland, Iceland, Scotland, Belgium, France, Switzerland, Spain, and Portugal; but there are no adequate histories.[36]

Because Louise Ritter came from Switzerland, it is important to review some of what is kown about Swiss immigrants to the United States. During the early 1880s migration overseas reached an unprecedented peak because Swiss farmers left their unprofitable farms to come to America. Swiss agriculture had suffered a series of disasters. In the mid-1840s it had been hurt by a potato pest, and this was followed by several failures of the grain crops in the early 1850s. These failures resulted in a decline of marriages and the birth rate. The Panic of 1857 hurt industries and Swiss exports. For a brief time in the 1860s, the economic conditions improved because of trade treaties. Then in 1873, another panic hit the world and ended free trade. Western markets were flooded with cheap grains from Eastern Europe and overseas. During the 1880s there were many farm bankruptcies. Swiss farmers were forced to shift from producing grain to dairying and cattle raising. This change was a slow and difficult process, especially since dairy exports met with protective tariffs of foreign countries where the same agricultural crisis had developed. The agricultural depression lasted almost twenty years. Conditions did not begin to improve until the 1890s.[37] The number of Swiss emigrating decreased after 1890, but up until World War I many Swiss continued to go abroad in search of prosperity.[38] Most of the Swiss immigrants to the United States came from agricultural or forestry groups and many were from the Bern area. They came for many of the same reasons other immigrants came – shortage of land, agricultural crises, and a developing machine technology which was dislocating farmers and craftsmen.

During their first years of marriage, Louise and Fritz Ritter had rented land and lived in Grafenried, Canton Bern, Switzerland. Here their sons had been born. At the time they decided to come to the United States, they were living in Iffwyl, a village of under 1500 persons in a little valley near Bern. They had no hope of ever being able to own farm land. Much of the Swiss sense of freedom is based on private ownership of property,[39] and a Swiss peasant could have cultural stability only if he remained in his community. His independence in that community depended on ownership of his house and land.[40] If a family had to move frequently to find jobs or land, the children could not have a sense of community citizenship; the sons would not have real cultural or economic stability and would continue as landless and economic outsiders. Louise Ritter's children would have been such outsiders in Switzerland.

One reason little is recorded about the Swiss in America is the language problem. Four-fifths of the total Swiss immigration was composed of Swiss-Germans.[41] Carl Wittke stated that it was not always easy to distinguish between Swiss, Dutch, Germans, and Russian-Germans since all of them represented geographical and national divisions which were far more important than differences in their cultural patterns. Because of language similarities, they were frequently confused, and exact statistics concerning their immigration are difficult to get.[42] Another source confirms this, stating that American immigration statistics long confused the Swiss-Germans and Swiss-French immigrants with people from Germany and France.[43] It is easy to understand the confusion of the native born Americans in regard to the language, but one wonders at the assertion that the national divisions were more important than the differences in cultural patterns.

Four-fifths of all Swiss are of peasant stock. They may have become urban dwellers, but they have not forgotten the challenges nature flung at their ancestors.[44] Because there are few natural resources in the country, the people have worked under limitations which developed qualities that have become their second nature. They are hard working, tenacious, frugal, and thrifty. They developed the ability to see possibilities where others see nothing.[45] For the Swiss, his country is a lifelong challenger. He loves his country "as a warrior loves an honest but pitiless adversary."[46]

While it is true that the topography and climate of Switzerland was a force in shaping the national character, the interior religious conflicts also shaped the character and future of the country. Acceptance of the Reformation in 1528 was a source of wealth. The Church property was seized in most Protestant countries, but in Switzerland it was not used for wars but held in trust for the people.[47] The Reformation also contributed to the Swiss work ethic. Labor was important for economic reasons, but it was also a challenge. Reformation meant not the elimination of the church's control over everyday life, but rather the substitution of a new form of control.[48] The God of Calvinism demanded of his believers not single good works, but a life of good works combined into a unified system.[49] The Reformation seems to have developed certain characteristic virtues and abilities. Among the upper classes, banking and finance, next to theology, became a type of work which was acceptable and rewarded. Among the lower classes, cotton spinning and weaving often replaced agriculture as the calling.[50]

The Catholic cantons resisted the nationalist movement for Swiss unification, but it was their stubborn tradition that left the deepest imprint on Swiss nationalist feeling. Through these pastoral cantons Swiss have maintained a link with their origins. Neither feudalism nor the state have ever been effective in subjugating the Swiss peasantry. The William Tell legend may not be a historical fact but an apocryphal tale, but it is a vital factor in the national consciousness of Switzerland. The people do not make changes easily. There is extreme political conservativism which is the conservatism of the mountain peasant.

National unity in Switzerland did not come from preferences of the people nor from the thinking of an elite group. It was imposed on the country by economic realities.[51] Switzerland's present constitution was adopted in 1874. The nation is a union of twenty-five cantons whose sovereignty is slightly wider than that of the states of the United States. The legislative branch has two chambers, and they elect for a four-year term the members of the executive branch. The "president" of the Swiss Confederation is a board of seven men, one selected from them each year to act as the nominal president. Most cantons have similar constitutions. Swiss citizenship is dual – federal and cantonal – and independent of residence. This applies to canton citizenship and national citizenship. Those who emigrate maintain Swiss citizenship unless they specifically request to have it revoked. Since every elector is a legislator and absence from the polls is punishable by a fine, the

9

result is the best educated electorate in the world.[52] Women did not have the vote in 1893, and they still do not, although many Swiss women have professions and hold positions of importance. Traditionally, the Swiss woman's role has been clear. She has been in charge of the home, and her rewards for dedication and hard work have been pride in her house and in her family.

One way to understand a nation is through its favorite sports. The Swiss enjoy mountain climbing, a sport which requires a team. The ethical code for mountain climbers must be one for all and all for one. All social distinctions disappear. The discipline is democratic rather than military. The leader is a servant, and the followers obey because they owe discipline to the rest. Alone they could not have the experience, so they work together and enjoy separately.[53] The Swiss are democratic, and they recognize the need for discipline and cooperation.

Along with their frugality and hard work, the Swiss people have acquired a reputation for humanitarianism. Their role in the Red Cross and their offering homes for refugees in two world wars prove their generosity. Since 1840, history records the nation's attempts to maintain neutrality and the continuing neutral position it wishes to maintain in the world. All of the character traits of the Swiss people appear in the character of Louise Ritter as it is revealed in her letters.

Louise Ritter spoke Schweitzerdeutsch. The Swiss have four national languages – German, French, Italian, and Romansch. The first three are official, meaning that all state papers must be translated into the three official languages. German is not a spoken but a written language. The spoken language, Schweizerdeutsch, is largely unintelligible to anyone but a Swiss-German. It is a branch of Alemannic, spoken in Switzerland and southern Germany for more than a thousand years. It is also distinguished from "dialect" in its ordinary meaning because it is spoken by all Swiss-Germans regardless of class or education.[54] The Swiss-Germans consider their language an important means for preserving the nation's cultural and political independence.

The Ritters did not come to a "New Switzerland" when they came to Nebraska. They did not have the large warm social group to come to which Swedes in Stromsberg or Czechs coming to Dwight or Prague, Nebraska, found. By 1900, there were only thirty-one Swiss in the area to which they came. According to Carl Wittke, the most important Swiss colonies still in existence in the United States in 1887 were in Illinois, Tennessee, West Virginia, Georgia, Kentucky, and Columbus in Platte County, Nebraska.[55] New Glarus, Wisconsin, still maintains its Swiss culture; and parts of Ohio have place names indicating settlement by Swiss. Of course, there was Sutter of California gold rush fame, who was later joined by many Swiss immigrants. However, the author of these letters came to an area of Nebraska with so few Swiss settlers that it is not listed as a Swiss settlement. The entire state of Nebraska had only 2,542 Swiss settlers in 1890.[56] In view of the tight character of Swiss society and the importance of the village, Louise and Fritz must have felt a peculiarly deep disruption from all that was familiar when they joined the 439,730 immigrants in the United States in 1893.[57]

Since it has been asserted several times that individual stories of humble people tell, at least partly, the story of immigration, it is necessary to look at the individual whose letters follow. As was mentioned, Louise Seigenthaler-Ritter came from Iffwyl, a small village in the Bernese Oberland, in 1893, with her husband and three small sons. She and her family spoke Schweizerdeutsch. She was able to write and speak the standard German learned at school. Her grandfather had been a medical doctor and her brother became a teacher. She was better educated than her husband. Her letters cover a thirty-two year period during which she attempted to keep her two countries and two families together.

The Ritter family left Switzerland for economic reasons – because they could not gain land at Iffwyl – and arrived in Tilden, Nebraska, in April of 1893. They settled on a farm three and a half miles west of Tilden in Antelope County. (See maps, p. 20). The local paper described the area as having "wondrous productive soil. Suffice it to say that Tilden is located in the very heart of Nebraska's choice garden spot." The description continued by enumerating the forty businesses located in this town with a population of 500. The farm land was further praised: "Land in this vicinity finds ready sale to eastern buyers at prices ranging from $16 to $39 per acre, owing to value of improvements. The farmers, with few exceptions, are out of debt, prosperous, contented and happy." The article included this evidence of success: "We may also add that Tilden exports more grain, cattle and hogs than any other point on the Elkhorn line west of Fremont."[58] Unfortunately for Louise and Fritz, Tilden did not live up to these promises. They arrived in the midst of a panic and drought, and the first six years tested their courage.

Local papers often played down the difficulties, hoping all problems would disappear. The author of a yearly report on Nebraska's progress granted there were some problems, but then concluded "the outlook is such as not to deter the persistent husbandman from continuing his work. In very many respects Nebraska has much for self-congratulation in comparison with other states."[59] Another contributor to the paper was more blunt:

> Without precedent 1893 was the worst in fifty years for business. The year 1893 was one of which not a great deal favorable can be said. It started with the largest trade ever known and business booming, but ended with the lowest prices on record and millions of men unable to secure employment.[60]

11

Louise and her family experienced the "dog years," Dorothy Skårdal's term for the period of painful adjustment which continued as long as an immigrant suffered considerable physical hardship.[61] Details in the Headnote for the first letter describe some of the problems they encountered their first years in Nebraska.

Louise and Fritz were too new to the country to become involved in the Populist movement which was a response to the economic hardships of the time, but her letters serve to record some of their difficulties during those early years of adjustment and economic insecurity. The papers carried the syndicated columns about the Spanish-American War, but few local people were involved.[62] Louise mentioned the Spanish-American War, but it had little direct effect on their lives. The Ritters were more concerned about the organization of a church and the too-short school term.

Louise kept an accurate record of the weather, different from what they had experienced before. Shortly after their arrival in Nebraska, an electrical storm terrified them. Some of those back in Switzerland must have felt she exaggerated, but in describing weather in the Great Plains it has never been necessary to lie. In a state where hailstones can weigh a pound, and where daily temperature increases of 40 degrees and 50 degrees have been recorded, and where temperatures have ranged from -48 degrees to 118 degrees, there is not much need for exaggeration.[63] Relatives of Louise who visited in Nebraska in June of 1974 kept a daily record of the temperature. Others asked if the wind ever stopped blowing. Certainly, it is impossible for the modern inhabitant of the Plains to understand the experience of the pioneer because of the radical change in the landscape. But Europeans and travelers from the eastern part of the United States still are unprepared for the space and extremes in weather they find in Nebraska. The same Swiss visitors several times just shook their heads and commented on what courage it took to come here. Three of them were the children of Anna, the sister to whom many of the following letters were written.

Louise had the "divided heart," and it is apparent in the tone of her letters. But she never isolated herself from the world; she was not provincial in her attitudes. Her letters show a continuing concern for world affairs. She followed the events in Europe which led up to World War I as carefully as she followed the market prices on their crops and livestock. She chided her Swiss family when she felt they were lacking in proper attitudes as she must have chided her American family. She had opinions and stated them.

The "dog days" of Louise and Fritz were left behind about 1901, and there was a brief period of comparative tranquility. Then a series of personal tragedies disrupted her peace. In the letters of 1902 and 1903 Louise shared her grief over the news of the death of her younger sister and the shock of the death of her son Rudolf, a baby when they immigrated. In these letters the reader follows her stages in dealing with the deaths and maintaining her

12

sanity. She told of the shock, disbelief, guilt, anger; the void that was left; the importance of the rituals of the funeral; her own desire for death. Her faith in God and the mercy of Christ enabled her to reach a level of resolution. It will be noted that in later letters she makes many other references to death, but never again is there evidence of the same emotional involvement. She had reached her acceptance that death is a part of life.

The deaths in Switzerland and in Nebraska forced her to acknowledge that she was forever alienated – she could never return home in any capacity other than as a visitor. There had been too many changes. She could never be wholly of Nebraska because of the language difficulties and the occasional conflict of values. She did establish a new community with neighbors of Swiss descent and those members of the newly organized German church. Her family's success brought her satisfaction and pride. World War I disrupted the development of her life in Nebraska. She was concerned for those in Switzerland, and she and her family were subjected to insult because of their language. The Yankees were unable to distinguish between Germans and Swiss.

After the war, she was an old woman, not so much chronologically, but physically. She continued to plead with the Swiss family to come visit or live near them. The tone of her letters indicates that she still cared, but it was difficult to write to those who were virtual strangers to her. She had to accept that the old life was gone forever. She would never return to Switzerland, none of her family would come to Nebraska, and the next generation would not know the Swiss language and culture. She could find satisfaction in the success of her sons, in their children, and the new house in town. Her religious faith enabled her to endure and prevail.

Undoubtedly, she would have agreed with some lines from Archibald Macleish's "American Letter":

It is a strange thing – to be an American . . .

America is neither a land nor a people,
A word's shape it is, a wind's sweep –
America is alone:
Only the taught speech and the aped tongue.
America is alone . . .

It is strange to sleep in the bare stars and to die
On an open land where few bury before us: . . .[64]

[1]The travel contract stated the agreement included transportation of persons and their luggage from Bern via Le Havre to Southampton and from there to New York under the following conditions: by railway third class from Bern, March 22, to the seaport and, March 25, by ship second class from Southampton to New York on the *City of Paris* of the American Line as well as by train from New York to Tilden, Nebraska. Fifty kilos were allowed for each child under twelve and 100 kilos for each adult. The infant traveled free of charge.

[2]The land abstracts show one previous owner of the land. No further information is available on the owner who sold his land, house, and furnishings.

[3]Maldwyn Allen Jones, *American Immigration* (Chicago: University of Chicago Press, 1960), p. 1.

[4]Robert A. Divine, *American Immigration Policy, 1924-1952* (New Haven: Yale University Press, 1957), pp. 24-25.

[5]Jones, pp. 275-277.

[6]Marcus Lee Hansen, *The Immigrant in American History* (Cambridge, Massachusetts: Harvard University Press, 1948), p. 191.

[7]Hansen, p. 68.

[8]Ibid.

[9]George M. Stephenson, *A History of American Immigration* (Boston: Ginn & Co., 1926), p. 10.

[10]William S. Bernard, Carolyn Zeleny, and Henry Miller, eds., *American Immigration Policy* (New York: Harper & Brothers, 1950), p. 8.

[11]Ibid., p. 299.

[12]Stephenson, p. 4.

[13]Oscar Handlin, *The Uprooted* (Boston: Little, Brown and Co., 1951), p. 5.

[14]Ibid.

[15]Ibid., p. 6.

[16]Theodore Blegen, *Grass Roots History* (Minneapolis: University of Minnesota Press, 1947), p. 7.

[17]Henry Steele Commager, "Introduction," *Immigration and American History* (Minnapolis: University of Minnesota Press, 1961), pp. 4-5.

[18]William S. Bernard, *Americanization Studies* (Montclair, New Jersey: Patterson Smith, 1971), p. 93.

[19]Ingrid Semmingsen, "Emigration and the Image of America in Europe" in *Immigration and American History,* p. 28.

[20]Theodore C. Blegen, *Land of Their Choice* (St. Paul, Minnesota: University of Minnesota, 1955), p. v.

[21]Hansen, p. 70.

[22]See maps on pp. 18-20.

[23]Walter Prescott Webb, *The Great Plains* (Boston: Ginn and Co., 1931), p. 505.

[24]Ibid., p. 507.

[25]Willa Cather, *O Pioneers!* (Boston: Houghton Mifflin Co., 1962), p. 171.

[26]Webb, p. 506.

[27]Dee Brown, *The Gentle Tamers* (Lincoln, Nebraska: University of Nebraska Press, 1958), p. 244.

[28]Oscar Handlin, "Preface," *The Divided Heart,* by Dorothy Burton Skårdal. (Lincoln, Nebraska: University of Nebraska Press, 1974), p. 7.

[29]Handlin, *The Uprooted,* p. 259.

[30]Ibid., pp. 259-260.

[31]Blegen, pp. 8-9.

[32]Dorothy Burton Skårdal, *The Divided Heart* (Lincoln, Nebraska: University of Nebraska Press, 1974), p. 91.

[33]Ibid.

[34]Ibid., pp. 24-25.

[35]*The Description of a Journey to My Native Country – Switzerland, and Return in 1913,* an unpublished travelog, p. 1. In the private library of Jeff Kappeler, Fremont, Nebraska.

[36]Carlton C. Qualey, "Prospects for Materials in Immigration Studies: in *Immigration and American History,* p. 131.

[37]Kurt B. Mayer, *The Population of Switzerland* (New York: Columbia University Press, 1952), pp. 31-36.

[38]Ibid., pp. 203-213.

[39]Daniela Weinberg, *Peasant Wisdom* (Berkeley: University of California Press, 1975), p. 26.

[40]Ibid., pp. 6-7.

[41]Carl Wittke, *We Who Built America* (New York: Prentice-Hall, Inc., 1940), p. 304.

[42]Ibid., p. 300.

[43]Mayer, p. 215.

[44]J. Christopher Herold, *The Swiss Without Halos* (New York: Columbia University Press, 1948), p. 148.

[45]Ibid., p. 208.

[46]Ibid., p. 148.

[47]Ibid., p. 103.

[48]Max Weber, *The Protestant Ethic and the Spirit of Capitalism,* trans., Talcott Parsons (New York: Charles Scribner's Sons, 1948), pp. 36-37.

[49]Ibid., pp. 114-115.

[50]Herold, p. 209.

[51]William Martin, *Switzerland from Roman Times to the Present,* trans. Jocasta Innes (London: Elek, 1971), p. 232.

[52]Herold, pp. 11-15.

[53]Ibid., pp. 15-151.

[54]Ibid., pp. 15-16.

[55]Wittke, pp. 300-301.

[56]John Paul Von Grueningen, ed., *The Swiss in the United States* (Madison, Wisconsin: Swiss-American Historical Society, 1940), p. 68.

[57]Bernard, Zeleny, and Miller, eds., p. 299.

[58]"The Pride of the Elkhorn," *Tilden Citizen,* 4 February 1893, p. 2.

[59]"Nebraska's Showing," *Oakdale Sentinel,* 27 January 1894, p. 2.

[60]*Oakdale Sentinel,* 6 January 1894, p. 3.

[61]Skårdal, p. 257.

[62]The *Tilden Citizen* from July 23, 1898 to August 27, 1898 includes no reference to local activity connected with the Spanish-American War.

[63]Roger Welsch, *Shingling the Fog and Other Plains Lies* (Chicago: The Swallow Press, Inc., 1972), p. 14.

[64]Sculley Bradley, et al, eds. *The American Tradition in Literature,* 3rd ed. (New York: W.W. Norton and Company, Inc., 1967), pp. 1338-1339.

15

Fritz and Louise Ritter's home in Iffwyl, Switzerland

NOTES ON THE MANUSCRIPT AND EDITING

In 1972, when Klara Wuthrich-Stucki gave me, Louise's granddaughter, most of the letters, she said that she and her family felt they now meant more to me than they would to anyone of the next generation in Switzerland. Several of the letters were circulated among the family for a last rereading before they were given to me. There are fifty-eight letters from the correspondence of Louise Seigenthaler-Ritter to her family from 1893 to 1925. The letters from the years 1893 and 1894 are in poor condition and have been laminated to preserve them. Some of the letters do not include her signature. Louise often added a small sheet of paper for an additional comment and her signature. Some of these are missing; otherwise, all but one of the letters appear to be complete. The letters were written in Old German script which cannot be read even by the younger Swiss. I am indebted to Maria Rosenblatt, retired German teacher and Professor Emeritus of Midland Lutheran College, for her transcription of the script.

The chronological order allows the reader to follow Louise's struggles with loneliness and homesickness as well as pride in the achievements of the family. The spelling of the family names has been changed to make it easier for the reader to follow references to the children. For example, when the children are small they are referred to as Fritzi, Ruedeli, Anneli, and Ernsti.[1] Fritz is her husband, and young Fritz becomes Fred in America. The other names are changed to Rudolf, Anna and Ernest. To make the letters easier to read, the material has been broken into paragraphs. Otherwise, the letters follow the original text. Explanatory information is included in introductory notes and footnotes to avoid detracting from Louise's account of her experiences as a pioneer immigrant woman in Antelope County, Nebraska.

---

[1]"The Swiss have made a success of thinking small. They have a habit of scaling everything down to minute size. Ringing through the Swiss-German language like perpetual baby chatter is the diminutive suffix *li.*" Herbert Kubly, *Switzerland* (New York: Time Inc., 1964), p. 146.

The diminutive ending, -*li,* is characteristic of many Swiss-German words, especially proper names. It is a mixture of French and German. J. Christopher Herold, *The Swiss Without Halos* (New York: Columbia University Press, 1948), p. 16.

SWITZERLAND

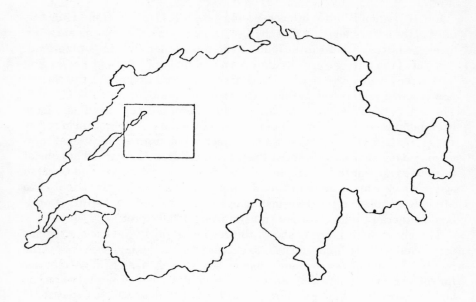

See the next page for enlargement of the area indicated on the map above.

Of special interest are the following towns and cities indicated on the enlarged map:

Mulchi – Louise's birthplace
Iffwyl – Ritter family's home before emigrating
Ins – Sister Anna's home

Other places indicated are frequently referred to in the text of the letters.

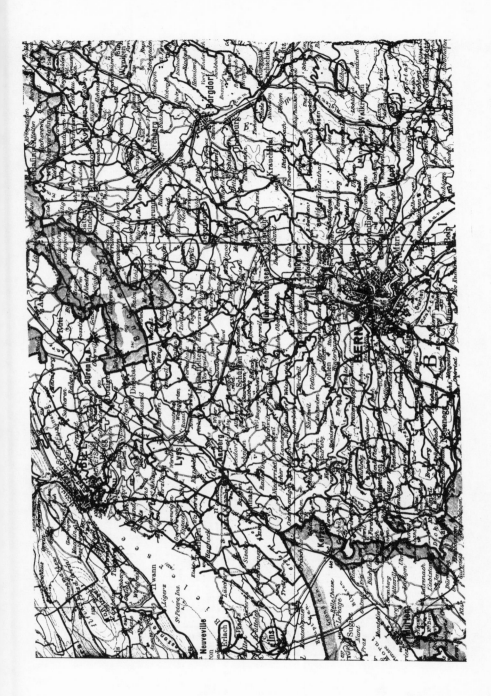

19

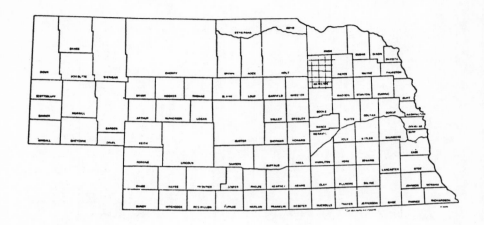

INTRODUCTORY NOTE

For Letter of August 27, 1893

This first letter reviews some of Louise and Fritz's early experiences in Nebraska. It should be remembered that they had made a train trip from Bern to LeHavre, from LeHavre to Southampton, followed by a long and uncomfortable ocean voyage. Oscar Handlin described the journey of the immigrants as "a succession of shattering shocks which conditioned the life of every man and woman that survived it."[1] The Ritters were on the ship from March 25 to April 9, and they were seasick during the eighteen days. Louise had to care for Rudolf, only three months old. Because their parents were too sick to supervise them, the older boys roamed the ship and were frequently in trouble with other passengers because of their mischief.[2] This experience was the Ritters' first contact with life as it was to be, learning to understand alien ways and alien languages, and managing to survive in a foreign environment. Their memories of the seasickness made both Louise and Fritz reluctant to return to Switzerland for a visit in later years.

Their journey was not ended with the arrival in New York. They still had to pass through Ellis Island, find a hotel, and board the train that would take them to Nebraska. Although there was a Rev. Paul H. Laud, who for years served as a missionary to the Swiss immigrants, meeting them on Ellis Island and then helping them to one of the Swiss hotels in New York,[3] there is no record that he helped this family.

After 1879 many special cars were built by the railroad companies to bring the immigrants west. The Ritter family might have traveled by ordinary day cars which contained benches without cushions and were heated by flat-topped stoves with which the passengers also heated their food and drink. At night they could have improvised the benches into bunks upon which they placed their own coats, shawls, or blankets to obtain minimal comfort.[4] Louise expressed no complaints concerning the train trip.

In the middle of April in 1893, the Fritz Ritter family arrived in Tilden, located in northeastern Nebraska. Because of disputes with the railroad, Antelope County had not begun to grow until after 1876. It then increased from 500 or 600 population to 4,552 in 1881.[5] The Ritter's farm was in Antelope County, three and a half miles west of Tilden. Because Jakob, Fritz's older brother, had come over in 1892 and bought the land and a furnished house, Louise had a comfortable home in which to settle herself and family.

Tilden, their town for trade and business, was located in Madison County, but it was closer than Neligh, the county seat of Antelope County. Tilden and the area around it were quite well settled in 1893. Within a radius of five miles were located four extensive horse and cattle ranches which bought,

21

fed, and shipped stock and created a local market for all kinds of farm produce. The railroad gave them direct communication with the Omaha, Sioux City, and St. Louis markets. The town of Tilden boasted the following businesses: two banks, seven general stores, two drug stores, three hardware stores, one boot and shoe store, one flour and feed store, one stationery and book store, two millinery stores, one hotel, four restaurants, two agricultural implement houses, one harness store, one jewelry store, one real estate office, one lawyer, one physician, two livery stables, one saloon, two lumber yards, two grain elevators, two blacksmith shops, one barber, two meat markets, and one newspaper.[6] It would be several years before the Ritters would visit the town to buy anything other than the necessities.

The Ritters had joined earlier immigrants from various parts of the world because of a hunger for land. In Switzerland, Fritz had worked for others as a tenant farmer and had been forced to move several times to provide for his growing family. There had been four sons born to them, one dying in infancy. Fritz had wanted to offer his children a better economic future than was available in Switzerland. Also, he was a proud man. Louise came from a family with land and a thriving business making cheese. He had wanted to offer her financial security. The only chance seemed to be in the United States. Descendants of Norwegian, Swedish, German, Dutch, Swiss, and British immigrants are found in great numbers in rural communities because they arrived in the United States at a time when abundant quantities of cheap and free land were still available. The land-grant railroads and the immigration bureaus of the northwestern states had concentrated their advertising campaigns on these groups because they were relatively prosperous groups who had members possessing the capital necessary to start American farming.[7] Fritz invested his little capital and borrowed money.

Louise's niece, Klara Stucki said of her aunt:

My mother told me often how her sister, your grandmother, was looking forward with great enthusiasm to the adventure, which it really was at that time and that no one could have stopped her from that plan. I am sure that the beginning in America was not easy for your grandparents. The strange, big country, the foreign language, and the separation must have weighed especially heavily on your grandmother.[8]

The letters support her statements. The beginning was not easy.

Loneliness was not the only problem they faced. They started their farming in the midst of a depression and a drought. A worldwide business depression had begun in Europe in 1890. This depression became a financial panic in the United States. In 1893 twenty-one banks failed in Nebraska and nearly all the remaining banks were upon the verge of collapse. Every farmer and every businessman lived from day to day in financial anxiety.[9] On May

13, 1893, C.G. Dawes, financier and future vice president, wrote in his journal that money matters over the country were assuming a very serious aspect. On May 22 he wrote that many failures were occurring and more were expected.[10] The financial situation did not ease the next year. Prices continued to fall, and increasing numbers of tramps wandered from farm to farm hunting a few days' work or a square meal.[11] The distress through the land was so severe that in March of 1894 Coxey's Army marched to Washington to demand relief.[12] Louise and Fritz Ritter started their lives in the state of Nebraska in the midst of the third major money panic and depression since Nebraska was born – (1857-59; 1873-79; 1890-99).[13]

Their "dog days" were more immediately caused by the drought. The drought in 1890, the first following statehood, was one of the driest years of the modern meteorological record. The years 1891 and 1892 brought considerably more moisture, but in the summers of 1893 and 1894 the drought returned.[14] In Nebraska there were almost total crop failures in 1893 and 1894. The state had only 16.26 inches of rainfall in 1893 and 13.54 in 1894; normal annual rainfall is 25.13 inches.[15] Then, "like an assaulting column under heavy machine gun fire the corn belt struggled through lengthening days of drought until July 26, when a furnace wind began to blow from the southeast." The Nebraska corn crop was dead in three days.[16] Dawes described July 26, 1894, as having savage winds and smoldering heat that lashed at humans, animals, and vegetation. The thermometer registered 105 degrees; the wind velocity was 40 miles an hour.[17] Everett Dick gives this description:

> In that awful holocaust corn blades shriveled in the blast like grass in an oven. Nebraska farmers stood helpless while their harvest was swept away by the relentless breath of the devastating simoon. All remaining hopes for the season dissipated in a single day.[18]

An unpublished history of Tilden records summer weather in the years 1892 through 1894 with temperatures ranging from 90 to 106 degrees. In 1894 there was no rain in July and August. Crops were a total loss. The years 1894-95 were known as the famine period. Vegetation was destroyed by hot winds in July. Many settlers were discouraged and left the vicinity.[19] According to the agricultural statisticians' report for October, 1894, the corn yield was fourteen percent of a normal corn yield.[20] Sheldon put it more strongly. He records the total state yield at about 14,000,000 bushels, grown on about 4,000,000 acres, the nearest to a complete crop failure in the state's entire history.[21] (Note that his report precedes the 1930s.) Mortgages and foreclosures and sheriff sales filled the newspaper columns.[22]

Louise and Fritz Ritter had not selected an ideal time to make their fortune in the United States.

My Dear Sister and Brother-in-law,

I enjoyed Anna's letter very, very much and would have answered it sooner, had I not waited in vain for a letter from home until now. If I could only chat with you about all that we enjoy and that depresses us, I would have so much to say.

The voyage and that we are now in America seems often like a heavy dream; and although I have it better here and nicer than over there, I still wish I could be with all my dear ones in our beautiful homeland. With God's will this great desire will come true one day that we will see each other again on this earth.

I do realize more and more that I could not have traveled at a better time with my dear ones than at that time. We were always favored by the other travelers, train personnel, and hosts, and no one objected to the warming of the milk for Rudolf with the ethyl alcohol lamp. Whereas, the family Mauch, who traveled with Uli,[23] were not allowed to warm the milk for their one-year-old child because of the danger of fire. Perhaps they had a lamp like you have.

In the Hotel Grutli in New York all ate with such good appetites that one would not believe that they had felt so miserable on the ship. The condensed milk and the later change to American milk did not bother the baby, quite the opposite. I never had a finer child than dear Rudolf.[24] Since the middle of May, I have not given him milk at night since he slept through it. During the day he is dear, drinks eagerly his bottle of milk and eats his zwieback which I bake for him from our beautiful white flour. We have no baker here. Every woman here bakes her own bread as well as she can. One has wide tables here and puts so much on them until they crack.

You will understand that we don't have it as comfortable as the ones who have been here for a long time. The meat is all gone, and it is too hot to be able to butcher. We could buy so much; we ought to spend money ten different places. Instead of buying, we kill chickens and make chicken soup, or we shoot rabbits which are here in abundance. In the spring we often saw three to four running over the field. There are also many pheasants and big and small prairie hens whose melancholy calls one can hear every day. Everybody here has the right to shoot what is on his land.[25] There are also snakes which horrify us. Just think, last Tuesday when Fritz plowed and didn't think of anything bad, he suddenly saw such a horrible snake in the field. He killed it, but the next day a still larger one fled into a mouse hole. There are many snakes on our land. Jakob says that he had never seen that many at Bernhard's.[26] They kill all they see, but the Yankees are not supposed to kill any. I saw one in front of the house door which frightened me terribly. They are not supposed to be poisonous and flee when they notice you, but the horror remains.

But I was scared of more than the snakes on Saturday, July 29, and the next night. If you had known it, your thoughts would have been with us more than ever. That afternoon, a colorful group with eight wagons came along the road and stopped at our house where our men were busy working. Jakob hurried to get some money; and when I asked him who they were, he said Indians. Afterwards I watched them secretly, these copper-brown fellows with their wives. There were four men, eight women, one half-grown fellow and a few smaller children. One I saw naked; he had red-brown skin. My fear was quite unnecessary; not one came to our house. They did beg from the men for several things and asked by pointing if they could pick cherries and stay overnight, which we of course allowed. So they pitched three tents and camped here overnight, hardly 200 to 250 steps from our house. No one can claim to have slept particularly well that night. The next morning, they departed early. They had seven horses. According to a paper, they came from Omaha and probably wanted to visit their people in the west.[27] If they want to return by train, the train company must transport them for free.

Now to something else. There is a special reason that I am writing everything without paragraphs. I don't want to send empty pages to Europe.

Now to the weather report and harvest prospects. We had an unusually dry summer and consequently the corn crop leaves a lot to be desired. This is mostly due to the scorching south wind. When it blows very hard, the poor plants will blow half away. Eight years ago, they say, the wind wilted the corn in one bad day. That tells a lot, since corn is such a strong plant. But men and animals also suffer badly. Our crop is not the worst; other farmers are worse off. In some places the corn looks good,[28] but if we will have a medium harvest in the end is to be seen. One cannot know that in advance with a field of 120 to 130 acres. Also in summer the wind blows hard. One is glad of it; otherwise the heat would be unbearable.

Lately we have had terrible thunderstorms, often the whole night through. The sky looked like fire, and the thunder rumbled constantly so that we trembled all the time. In the beginning of July a terrible flash frightened us so much that we thought the lightning must have hit the iron windmill a few steps from our house. Also in the night between the 18th and 19th there was a gruesome, beautiful electric storm. About midnight it stood directly over us. A terrible noise made us almost faint, and believing that our living room was on fire, we seized our dearest ones, our children, in our deadly fear. We were literally showered with fire. But the most dreadful did not happen. The Lord had been merciful with us. But we saw how close it had been the next morning. In the kitchen in the wall just below the loft behind the stove there was an enormous hole. The lightning must have gone down the pipe from the outside, for we saw on the outside that the lightning must have gone into the ground along a wire at the pipe. Yet I am not more afraid of storms than

25

before for: "When in storms the lightning's flash mountains shake, I trust in God's mercy."

Saturday, Sept. 2. This evening I want to finish my letter so that we can take it to town tomorrow when we go to church.[29] Perhaps there will be a letter there from home.[30] Do write me about the family when you know something of them, and don't wait as long as I did.

Our men folks finished the grape harvest today. We will have quite a good crop. We also preserved a barrel of wild plums. We will have to wait to see what they taste like. If we could make schnapps of all our plums on our land, we could make quite a fortune. All alcoholic beverages are about five times more expensive here than in Switzerland. The grapes grow wild here, often high up into the trees, so that grapes, plums and cherries form a whole roof — it is beautiful to see.

Father and you will have sold your cheese, and I hope that you are all having a good year.[31] I would be glad to hear from you. And now, to end with the best. Does your little boy Ernst Rudolf[32] also grow as happily as our little Rudolf? I do hope he is in good health. You will enjoy him so much; too bad that both are so far away from each other. Rudolf has been putting his big toe into his mouth for a long time, and for ten days he has had two teeth. Anna, do write soon again. I love to read letters from Switzerland, which unfortunately are so rare. If you think you should, show my letter to all the relatives. Give my greetings to all, especially to Grandmother in Biglen. Above all many thousand greetings to you all in our dear homeland and to the dear little ones.

Many kisses from your sister and sister-in-law.

L. Ritter

Fritz and Hans are well.

Farewell and be happy. God be with you every day until the end of the world. Amen.

[1]Handlin, *The Uprooted*, p. 38.

[2]Evidently Louise and Fritz had discussed their discomfort with their family. Fritz often told this story of their illness and the trouble the boys caused.

[3]*Einwanders Freund*, Cleveland, Ohio, February 1938.

[4]Robert G. Athearn, *Union Pacific Country* (Chicago: Rand McNally and Co., 1971), p. 180.

[5]*History of Antelope County 1883-1973* (Service Press, Inc., April 1976), p. 2.

[6]"The Pride of the Elkhorn," *Tilden Citizen*, 4 February 1893, p. 2.

[7]Maldwyn Allen Jones, *American Immigration* (Chicago: The University of Chicago Press, 1960), p. 210.

[8]Letter to the author from Klara Stucki of Ins, Switzerland, 4 April 1978.

[9]Addison Erwin Sheldon, *Nebraska: The Land and the People* (Chicago: The Lewis Publishing Co., 1931), I, p. 732.

[10]Charles G. Dawes, *A Journal of the McKinley Years*, ed. Bascom N. Timmons, (Chicago: The Lakeside Press, 1950), pp. 28-29.

[11]Sheldon, I, p. 738.

[12]Ibid., p. 737.

[13]Ibid., p. 740.

[14]Merlin P. Lawson, Kenneth F. Dewey, and Ralph E. Neild, *Climatic Atlas of Nebraska* (Lincoln, Nebraska: University of Nebraska Press, 1977), p. 54.

[15]James C. Olson, *History of Nebraska* (Lincoln, Nebraska: University of Nebraska Press, 1955), p. 239.

[16]Sheldon, I, p. 738.

[17]Bascom N. Timmons, *Portrait of an American: Charles G. Dawes* (New York: Henry Holt and Co., 1953), p. 36.

[18]Everett Dick, *Conquering the Great American Desert* (Nebraska Historical Society, 1975), p. 345.

[19]Mrs. Lucius Ives, "A History of Tilden," on file in Tilden Public Library.

[20]Dick, p. 349.

[21]Sheldon, I, p. 739.

[22]Ibid.

[23]Uli Whitwer was married to Fritz's sister Marianne. "When the rail net was completed to the Mississippi, the carriage of immigrants became an important feature. This business was sought by the railroads not only for the immediate revenue or the disposal of their lands, but for the more permanent income to be derived from settlement. Hence tickets were sold in the interior villages of Europe, alliances were formed with steamship lines, competition was bitter in the ports, and fares were reduced to ridiculous figures, as in the railroad war of 1885 when for a time the flat rate from New York to Chicago was only a dollar." Marcus Lee Hansen, *The Immigrant in American History* (Cambridge, Massachusetts: Harvard University Press, 1948), pp. 197-198.

[24]The youngest of their three children, born December 27, 1892.

[25]"Up to 1895 there were practically no game laws ... The prairie chicken was a prairie grass bird and lived only on the prairie, never in the woods." Pierce County joins Antelope County. This anecdote can be accepted or not. "Prairie chickens were so plentiful and so savage in the early days that on August 1, 1890 the Pierce County leader warned the townspeople not to venture out of town without a dog and a shot gun, and a boy to manage the team in case of a sudden attack by these blood-thirsty fowls." Esther Kolterman Hansen, *Along Pioneer Trails in Pierce County Nebraska,* 1940, pp. 60-61.

[26]Bernhard Whitwer came from Switzerland in 1858 and to Antelope County in 1869. Jakob worked for him when he first arrived in Nebraska in 1892.

[27]A trail used by Pawnees and Poncas in visiting back and forth was close to their farm. A.J. Leach, *The History of Antelope County, Nebraska* (Chicago: The Lakeside Press, 1909), p. 28.

Chapter 3 of the unpublished "History of Tilden" states: "Indians were frequently around the town. They were copper-colored, tall and straight, with long black hair. Their usual dress was a band about the waist and an apron to the knees – buffalo robe and moccasins .... At that time the Pawnee, a powerful and warlike tribe were the most numerous in the Burnett vicinity." (Burnett was first name given Tilden.)

"In 1890 Poncas and Sioux made peace and the Sioux gave back to the Poncas part of their old lands on the Niobrara. About one-third of the tribe came back, the remaining staying in the Indian Territory." Addison Erwin Sheldon, *History and Stories of Nebraska* (Lincoln, Nebraska: University Publishing Co., 1929), p. 174.

It is impossible to state definitely what tribe of Indians these would have been. There are frequent references to Sioux parties stealing horses, etc. However, these do not seem to fit that tradition. The practice was to just speak of "Indians" when describing groups in the vicinity. It is most likely these were Omaha Indians.

[28]Prices for crops were as follows: wheat - 40¢, corn - 27¢, eggs - 10¢ a dozen, hogs - $6.00. *Oakdale Sentinel,* 29 July 1893, p. 1.

[29]At this time they attended the German Lutheran church.

[30]Rural delivery began in 1902. *History of Antelope County,* p. 3.

[31]Louise's father and brother-in-law were both cheese makers.

[32]First child of her sister Anna, born in 1893.

Louise Ritter-Siegenthaler's wedding picture

INTRODUCTORY NOTE

For Letters of October 22 and Christmas, 1893

The first months were busy, and the entire family was involved in the farming and harvesting. Machines were already an important part of the farming scene. Louise shared with her relatives her fascination with their efficiency.

She used the word "Yankee" to refer to native-born Americans. This was typical of the newcomers; the name was used both in praise and as a judgment.[1] The first contacts between Americans and immigrants produced a degree of antagonism because of the element of strangeness and the differing degrees of moral worth attached to given values, as viewed by Americans, on the one hand, and by immigrants, on the other.[2] This term also served as a negative reference for the German and Swiss immigrants in Nebraska to reveal what they opposed and what they favored. The immigrant often thought the Yankee was industrious enough, but his energies were frequently misdirected. He was frugal enough, yet he was also wasteful of the resources of his farmland.[3] Her first judgment of the Yankees condemned their callous treatment of their cattle.

Louise was not completely isolated from Switzerland. Some settlers in the area were earlier arrivals from Switzerland, and among them were relatives of her husband. Platte County, Nebraska, had been settled earlier by many Swiss. Visits with these fellow exiles from her homeland helped to dispel some of the loneliness. But she missed her family in Switzerland and began her years of coaxing and asking them to visit or join her.

The first Christmas in Nebraska must have been a difficult time for the entire family.

Tilden, Oct. 22, 1893

Dear Ones,

More than six weeks have passed since I received your letter, and I didn't think then that I would let you wait so long. It was Tuesday when Fritz went to Tilden in the evening, and the next day threshing began. That same evening I had threshers for supper, and they stayed overnight. We only had to thresh half a day, but we had much grain. The same week this threshing machine threshed at Uli's three brothers. The machine is driven by steam. Swiss farmers would look at this machine as a miracle. Everything is quickly threshed and cleaned, yet not more than eleven men are needed. When it has finished in one place, it is hooked to an engine and taken to another place where it will reduce to empty straw heaps the bundles of grain, this greedy monster. On either side of the man who puts in the bundles stand two men who cut the bands. The cleaned grain goes directly into the wagon, and two men drive it home and shove the grain out. Having the grain threshed cost us about eight dollars or twenty-four francs. We only have to pay the four men[4] who go with the machine; the others share help with us. These four are part of the total of eleven it takes to do the work.

I have to add something about the harvesting. When one has seen the master work done by those machines, it is well worth telling others about it. To harness three horses and sit and call "hu!" and let four or five bundles fall down together is really something great rather than employing a host of threshers and having to pay not less than a hard dollar daily. High wages make everything expensive that has to be done by hand.

But back to the harvesting. After the grain was harvested, I did not have to set one foot in the fields. In the morning, not as early as over there where we had to get up before sunrise, the mowing machine and men with the horse rake came. Much of the hay has already been stored.

It was very hot and dry this summer, and even the oldest men could not remember such a summer. So you see, it was not much different from the weather in Europe. However, there is no worry about feed for the cattle. We had heavy thunder storms – you may have read the letter which I wrote to Sister Anna about five weeks ago.

As to the Indians who settled close to us, don't worry. Many are better than many a white man, and they don't bother us. Now we have seen Indians face to face, and I am certain many would love to see them also, perhaps wishing them behind bars.

My dear ones, I hope you are not angry with me because I have not written for so long. I was always so busy, and the main reason is that I was very worried about our corn harvest which is now in full swing. When I wrote you last, the cornfields were exceptionally beautiful, but then because of the scorching south wind and lack of rain, the leaves hung down limp and withered. The corn could not properly set on those high stalks. There are some beautiful ears, but many are underdeveloped. But, as said before, we have enough food and the yield is better than expected.

Grandfather and Grandmother, aunts and uncles, all would enjoy the boys if they could see how cheerfully they help with the corn and potatoes. The potato crop is very good. They often get quite expensive. Last spring we could have earned much if we had been able to sell the potatoes from fall. They get expensive because the Yankees are too lazy to plant them. In Columbus, Nebraska, where Uli's Elise worked last summer, the people bought potatoes in paper sacks. In that town are many Swiss people.[5] Nine men and two women came here to Bossards for a visit. They emigrated twenty years ago as poor servants and now they own fine farms. They also visited us, and we could talk about the dairy and cheese making. I am supposed to write my father that Wilhelm Ernst von Aarange (the man's name) had heard a woman say she knew best how to make cheese.[7] There was a lot of laughter. What do you think dear Father? The cheese are not nearly as good as yours. I thought Uli's best here in America. The Americans dye it so it looks yellow.

I cannot think of anything nicer than that you, my dear ones, would come here in the spring. There were many older people with us crossing the ocean. Emma[8] could earn good money. Two dollars per week is the lowest wage here. In large cities they earn much more. But if you didn't like it here, you would be homesick.

Tilden, Christmas 1893

To all my Dear Ones, Parents, Brothers and Sisters,

Now we are standing at the threshold of the year 1894. We have experienced much in the year which soon will be gone. We turned our backs to our dear and beautiful homeland with all you beloved ones in order to found a new home here in the foreign land. But I can never be really happy although we are getting along all right; it is the homesickness that will plague me here in America. I wish and hope that you all over there can celebrate a Merry Christmas and enter in the best of health in a week's time a happy and peaceful New Year. I hope from all my heart that now while writing this letter our dear father is recuperating and able to celebrate the New Year with a joyous and grateful heart. Do take good care of yourself, dear Father, for when a letter from you arrives, and I learn that you are all well that is the greatest joy for me.

The past week, we all were not very well but are better now. It is best to stay well, for it is far to a doctor, and they don't come to the house for less than three to four dollars. Even to pull a tooth costs a half dollar. Your letter arrived the day before yesterday; Elisabeth's the Wednesday before. Also, Sister Anna wrote me recently. When you see her, please give her my greetings and best wishes for the New Year, also to brother Fritz. I would enjoy hearing from him soon.

We have been having severe winter weather since yesterday. A week ago the weather was mild and beautiful. Saturday night it rained heavily, and then it froze. Last night was very stormy, especially bad for the poor animals which rarely have a shelter here in America.[9] We have only a barn for the horses; all the other animals must stay outside. But now we have also made arrangements for the cattle against the hardship of the weather. Today there is a sight which I have never seen before. The trees up to the smallest twigs are covered with ice, also every blade of grass. The sun shines now on it all and offers a colorful spectacle – grimly beautiful. It gets colder here than in Switzerland, but fortunately it doesn't last more than two to three days. One day it may turn so warm that we can be outside in shirt sleeves, and the next day it can be so cold that one cannot put on enough clothes.

31

Since November Fred[10] has attended the English school, forty minutes away from here. Father usually takes him and brings him home. When the weather is mild, they walk. He likes school and can say the alphabet and read it and count to a hundred. Last Friday all pupils got some candy from their teacher. She gets thirty-two and a half dollars monthly. There is no apartment in the school. She lives close to her parents. Fred wants to write you an English letter later.

At night we often hear wolves.[11] It is quite gruesome since there are often so many together. They are supposed to not harm people. Only twenty minutes from us is the Northwestern Pacific[12] railroad. There is much freight transported; sometimes one freight train after another. We have even seen four passing through in Tilden. Often there is one coach hooked on to the freight train for passengers. Traveling in them is not pleasant. We once went in one from Tilden to Norfolk; it nearly threw us off our seats.

Dear Father, we are very glad that you can lend us the money. We think it best if you send it through Zwilchenbartle.[13] He will give you a receipt and send us a check which we will receive in a week's time. It was like that when we sent the money a year ago. Jakob got the check in about four weeks. As soon as we receive the money, I'll send you the receipt. Remember, Fritz paid 520 fr. for the dollars, including the postage. If possible, send the money immediately so that we receive it before February 15. Fritz wants to pay back the one hundred dollars which we borrowed from the bank before then.[14]

I am closing with many greetings from all of us, and with best wishes for the New Year. Happiness, health and God's richest blessings be with you. Your grateful Louise Ritter Siegenthaler, Fritz and children.

Don't be afraid that we will let Rudolf freeze. We heat well, and at night he sleeps with me or Hans.[15] We have large beds. Thanks again for the good, warm blanket. Greetings to my aunts.[16] Also those in Biglen and Bernhards. We enclose two stamps for Mr. Russi. We'll send more later. Happy New Year!

[1]Philip D. Jordan, "The Stranger Looks at the Yankee," in *Immigration and American History,* p. 69.

[2]Bernard, *Americanization Studies,* p. 24.

[3]Jordan, pp. 55-78.

[4]"It took a four man crew to operate the straw-burner – a separator man, an engineer, a fireman, and a water hauler." Dick, *Conquering the Great American Desert,* p. 313. Farmers at the central and western states moved from hand binding of the Marsh machine invented after 1858 to automatic binding device which would free two or three men from each harvester. In 1873 wire binders came into use. The wire had to be cut from the bundle before threshing, and if one slipped through it could damage the machine or endanger cattle. In 1870 the During Company marketed George Appleby's twin binder which increased the amount of grain a farmer could harvest. By 1880 the self-binder became a success and replaced the wire binder. Refine-

ments in the threshing machine increased its capacity and cleanness, added steam power, self-feeders, and straw stackers. It became both efficient and safe after 1878. Fred A. Shannon, *The Farmer's Last Frontier, Agriculture, 1860-1897* (New York: Rinehard & Company, Inc.), pp. 134-137.

Using the hand cradle in 1830 a man could harvest twenty bushels of grain in sixty-one hours; in 1900 the same amount of work could be done in less than three hours. Samuel Eliot Morison, Henry Steele Commager, and William E. Leuchtenberg, *The Growth of the American Republic,* 6th ed. (New York: Oxford University Press, 1969), II, p. 126.

[5]Nebraska did have a population of native Swiss: 1870 - 593; 1890 - 2,542; 1900 - 2,340; 1920 - 1,808. Von Grueningen, ed., *The Swiss in the United States,* pp. 58 and 68. Many settled in Platte County. "In 1885 more than a third of the potential voting population of Platte County was of German stock. Included with the German community were the largest Swiss German and Austrian German groups within the state . . . . A German Reformed congregation reflects the Swiss origin of many of the people." Frederick C. Luebke, *Immigrants and Politics* (Lincoln, Nebraska: University of Nebraska Press, 1969), p. 99. Outside of Douglas County, Platte and Sheridan – "Old Jules" area – had the most Swiss settlers. Douglas had 267 in 1890 and 241 in 1920; Platte 397 in 1890 and 231 in 1920; Sheridan 105 in 1890 and 68 in 1920. There are no statistics for Antelope County. Von Grueningen, ed., p. 55.

[6]Emanuel and Elisa Bossard were earlier arrivals from Switzerland. Bernard Whitwer was the brother of Elisa and was instrumental in bringing the Bossards and others of the family to the Tilden area. He had also employed Fritz's brother Jakob when he first arrived in the Tilden area in 1892. *Rooted in Faith,* 75th Anniversary book of Peace United Church of Christ, Tilden, Nebraska, 1977, p. 37.

[7]The cheese they made was Emmental, named for the valley of the Emme in the Bernese Oberland. There were many other varieties, both soft and hard. Herold, *The Swiss Without Halos,* p. 122.

[8]Emma was the sister next to Louise in age. She was twenty-eight years old when Louise and Fritz left Switzerland. (See Appendix I for clarification of family relationships.)

[9]In Switzerland cows are kept in barns in the valleys. Early in the summer they are driven to lower grazing lands. Herold, p. 123. The Bernese farm house often was constructed to include cattle and people under the same roof.

[10]Their oldest son, who was six years old.

[11]It is quite possible that there were wolves and not coyotes that they heard at this time. "The animal that has been killing young cattle up near the head of the Clearwater was killed last Saturday, and instead of a mountain lion it proved to be a monster grey wolf. It stood thirty-two inches high and measured six feet from the tip of its nose to the end of its tail, and across its forehead measured eight inches." *Oakdale Sentinel,* 29 July 1893, p. 1. Leach in *History of Antelope County* refers to prairie wolves killing deer, p. 21. A family history from an area near, New Helena, has this entry: "Did I tell you there are wild animals here? Bears, panthers, mountain lions and two kinds of wolves." The entry was on February 8, 1880. Berna Hunter Chrisman, *When You and I Were Young Nebraska* (Broken Bow, Nebraska: Purcell's Inc., 1971), p. 33.

[12]There must be an error in her name for the train. According to the unpublished history of Mrs. Lucius Ives, the Fremont, Elkhorn and Missouri Valley Railroad Company owned the track in 1879. Many others refer to it as the Chicago and Northwestern. Leach's history records the Omaha and Northwestern owned the greater part of the land and sold it to the Chicago, St. Paul, Minneapolis and Omaha – a part of the Chicago and Northwestern. Later this became the Burlington and Missouri. There were two state lines, Midland Pacific and Sioux City and Pacific. James C. Olson, *History of Nebraska* (Lincoln, Nebraska: University of Nebraska Press, 1955), p. 160. It is not difficult to understand how she might have confused the name. She must have meant the Chicago Northwestern line.

[13]Colloquial name. Probably a local banker.

[14]During the "dog years" or difficult beginning years they received the help from Louise's parents in Switzerland. Interview with Ernest Ritter, December 1978.

[15]Hans was the four year old son.

[16]Louise's mother came from a large family of five sons and seven daughters. These were the aunts she greeted.

33

The winter allowed time to relax, but it also gave them time to think about what they had done. They were now out of their traditional environment and replanted in strange ground, among strangers, where strange manners prevailed. The customary modes of behavior were no longer adequate, since the problems of life were new and different. They faced the enormous problem of working out new meaning to their lives, often under harsh and hostile circumstances.[1] The new land did not reward them for their hard work. Instead they discovered the violence and extremes in the weather in this strange land where they did not even care enough about the livestock to provide shelter for them.

The history of immigration is a history of alienation and its consequences. Louise had time to reflect on the broken family circle, her separation from known surroundings, the becoming of a foreigner and ceasing to belong. Her heart was partly with her people in Switzerland, but she was living in Nebraska. Her loneliness was caused by more than being severed from family. There was a sense of isolation because back in Switzerland the village had given her a sense of place. In the new country, all this was gone; that was hard enough. Harder still was the fact that there was nothing to replace this loss. Fortunately, they were able to visit with some of their neighbors; and rather than brooding on what was lost, they began building a new community.

January 28, 1894

Dear Sister and Brother-in-law,

I just wrote to Elisabeth in Jagenstorf, and now I want to write to you. I am very annoyed that almost all to whom we have written had to pay extra postage. Therefore, I will make this letter short. It is a pity that we can't talk to each other, for I would like to know how everything is in Batterkinden, if you sold the milk and to whom. Also, I would like to know about Father's plan – if he plans to buy milk again or if our parents want to come to Nebraska. I can hardly expect that, although it would give me so much joy. If it would happen, I could hope that you also would follow them into the new world. You could become our neighbors; those south and north are thinking of selling. But you would hardly think of it for this year, and so I wish you and your young household the very best from all my heart. If your little boy continues to progress so much, he will be well ahead of our dear little Rudolf, for he doesn't want to stand on his fat legs, but it does not matter. I very much hope that your dear little one is in good health, and that you also, dear Sister and Brother-in-law Ernst. He should also write one day.

At Christmas I heard from Sister Emma that Father was sick, but I hope he has recovered already. It worries me much to hear from such a distance that one in the family is sick. But I love to hear that all are well. Is our dear Mother well? I hope so, so she can assist you in your grave hour.[2] You are close to dear relatives; greetings to all in Biglen and Weyergut. The green coat which I bought in Biglen has worn well.

Before New Year's Day it was very cold, especially on Christmas Day, but we also had friendly and sunny days. After Christmas until January 20, the days were mild. But then it changed. Strong north winds blew over the land, and on Tuesday there was a terrible snow storm. It is so cold that it almost bites away the skin. Just to feed the chickens, I put on a coat and wrapped my head with a shawl and still almost died from the cold. After such days are over, one can hardly believe they were so cold. The newspapers said that many cattle died on those days. You should know that here in this barbaric land the cattle have no warm refuge in stables.[3] There are people who try to make you believe that the animals are used to the cold weather and to ice on their backs. We have a barn for six horses, and a mediocre cow stable. We also have a shelter with spaces with four wooden boards over which branches and straw and dirt are laid as a roof. This is bad in wet weather, but otherwise good enough. There are no doors, for no one fastens these intractable bulls which we have been fattening for a week. Before that we had them in the corn fields where they had plenty of food.[4] Unfortunately, we had to slaughter one because of constipation. It had wonderful meat. I remember that they say over there that American meat is not so tasty; we find it more the opposite.

There is not much work now, and we never before could stay in bed as long as we have this winter. Rarely do we arise before eight o'clock. That is the custom here. The American farmer has an easier life. Every day he has meat, butter and white bread as well as cake and cookies. But there is nothing like home, our dear Fatherland. Hearty greetings from Fritz and the children. All the best and write soon. Your sister and sister-in-law,
Louise Ritter

Tilden, February 8, 1894

My dear Parents, Brothers and Sisters,

This morning your dear letter arrived which we had been waiting for since last Saturday. On Saturday Gottfried brought us the check, and the same afternoon Fritz took it to the bank. We think the money can arrive by Saturday or Monday, so soon the letter and receipt will be sent to you. But, dear Father, don't worry about 1800 francs being less than 400 dollars. How could we be angry with you because of this misunderstanding? We are happy and grateful to have received this much. Fritz thinks you will receive the receipt which we are going to send to Zwilchenbart. If not, do write to us and we will send one immediately. The dollar is equal to 5.24 francs, and we will receive $381.60. I think he sent the money quickly so that you cannot say anything about it. For 5.20 francs it would have yielded three dollars more. The letter will be mailed today, February 12.[5]

My main wish is that you are well, and from all my heart I hope that you, dear Father, are fully recovered at this time. So take good care of yourself and don't go out in this cold weather. I must honestly say that I am happier if you don't buy any milk,[6] since that is so very expensive and it is very uncertain how the cheese trade will turn out. Also, dear Father, you can then take better care of yourself. I hope you find a place to live which you will like. Emma will most likely stay with you if she does not marry. Then she will have a good opportunity to do her needlework.

It is a pity that you don't live closer, for then you, dear Emma, could earn a good bit of money this summer. Elise Whitwer, Marianne's[7] oldest daughter, has worked in Oakdale since December. She washes the dishes, sweeps twice a week and gets three dollars a week. But for that, I don't want to encourage you to come here because there is nothing nicer than Switzerland. I also believe that you dear Parents would not be happy here. In good weather we go visit someone on Sundays unless someone comes to us. We don't have that cozy living here and the language is different. Uli's[8] three brothers all have German wives, and they speak High German instead of Swiss-German.[9] We also visit with Bossards and Stuckis. On New Year's Day Bossards came and got us so that we could celebrate the day with them. Bossard asked me to send his greetings, although he does not know you. And I am to tell you that we are not lost here. They are less formal here than abroad. They asked us to say "du" to them.[10] Last week Peter and his friend were here, and they brought us sauerkraut. Peter also said, "You must say 'du' to me."

Dear Mother, you asked if I never wrote your brother in Ohio.[11] Unfortunately I lost his address. Please send it to me in your next letter. Fritz has asked me often to write and ask him how it is there, for he does not like it here very much. If only we hadn't so much wind here. In the winter we had calm days, but when the wind blows, it is as if it even came through all the walls.[12] You remember how I described Christmas to you to show how icy it was here? Then it got milder, and until January 20 we had friendly days. On January 20, the wind began to blow, and then it turned terribly cold, and we had a blizzard. Many cattle died, for here the cattle have to be in the open day and night, summer and winter. It is terrible. And it is so hard on the poor people who have not enough to eat and no warm clothes and heating material. We are fortunate to have enough. We have wood and corn cobs. But many people here in Nebraska have no wood and no corn cobs; they have nothing but manure and straw to burn. We have very cold weather just now, but they

37

say these days don't last longer than three days.

You would like to have a picture of us, and we hope we can fulfill your wish.

[1]Handlin, *The Uprooted,* p. 5.

[2]Anna was her second sister, twenty-three years old at this time. Anna's second child, Fritz, was born in 1894. The eldest has been referred to before – Ernst, the only one of her nieces and nephews she ever saw.

[3]In Switzerland cows are kept in village stables all winter, from November to early May. Weinberg, *Peasant Wisdom,* p. 21.

[4]Prices for crops were not high: Wheat from 35 to 37¢; corn from 18 to 20¢ a bushel. *Oakdale Sentinel,* 26 August 1893, p. 3.

[5]There is no record of the financial arrangements. It is known that Fritz borrowed money from her parents so they could travel second class rather than steerage. They felt it would have been too difficult with the three small children. Then he had to borrow more money because of the problems the first three years.

[6]There was a world wide depression in 1893 and 1894. Switzerland was not immune to its effects.

[7]Marianne was one of Fritz's sisters, ten years older than he. They had come over several years earlier.

[8]Uli Whitwer was Marianne's husband and Elise's father.

[9]Swiss had and have little fondness for the German language, often preferring to flounder in French than to admit that they can understand or speak the German of Germany. Herold, *The Swiss Without Halos,* pp. 16, 17. But in the United States German must have sounded like home.

[10]The informal form of "you".

[11]Alfred Kunz, born in 1848, was Louise's mother's brother. He had immigrated to Columbus, Ohio, in 1868. Klara Stucki has the letters written by Alfred and his sister Anna Marie (who later returned to Switzerland) to their sister Margaretha Kunz-Rohrer. Since the death of her daughter Anna Rohrer in 1972, they have been in the possession of Klara Stucki. In the introduction, reference was made to the importance of family loyalties, no matter how distant. The importance of the letters is further substantiated by the second set being saved by the family.

[12]"The average wind velocity of the high plains of Nebraska and adjoining states is about 10 to 12 miles; 25 is not uncommon and a velocity of 40 miles and more is recorded a half-dozen or more times every year." Sheldon, *Nebraska The Land and the People,* I, p. 25.

INTRODUCTORY NOTE
For Letter of November 19, 1894

The second year of drought and resulting financial insecurity heightened Louise's sense of loneliness. Frederick Luebke, in *Immigrants and Politics,* divided immigrants into two groups: those whose psychological orientation was American and those whose cultural bonds continued to be with the land that gave them birth. The first type was characterized by a resolve to break with the past and to make a satisfactory adjustment to the new environment. By contrast, the European-oriented immigrants clung to memories of home. For such a person emigration exacted a sentimental loss that could never be replaced.[1] Rölvaag's Per Hansa and Beret Holm in *Giants in the Earth* illustrate the two orientations, but they represent extremes. The Beret Holm type symbolized slower assimilation, rural isolation, and preservation of Old World heritages.[2] Louise did not fit in either classification; she longed for home, but she was involved in the affairs of her family here in Nebraska – weather, crops, and prices. She was sustained by the hope that she would return to Switzerland in eight years.

Tilden, November 19, 1894

Dear Sister and Brother-in-law,

At last it is your turn again to write. I hope you are not angry that I have not written for so long. I know that our parents let you read the letters, so I don't want to bother you with my grievances. It is just like this: no crop, have to buy the feed, and always the same.[3] Thank God, we are well. We have to struggle through like thousands of others who may be even worse off than we. The great drought has spoiled our corn. Feed prices have gone up rapidly. For instance in the spring corn was 22 to 24¢ a bushel; now it is 55 to 58¢.[4] It is somewhat cheaper by the wagon bushel load – 400 weight. Last week Fritz bought a wagon load for 52¢ a bushel; today it is up again to 54¢. We also bought two tons of oil meal for the hogs and wheat flour. I tried to bake some bread with it, and I can assure you, it is as your half-white bread as to whiteness and quality.

We hope to be able to feed the corn and oil meal until the twenty-one cattle are shipped; then we will have only thirteen left. It will be a long time until something will grow, and we still have eighty hogs.

In regard to the high feed prices, the prices for fat hogs are too low. We hope that they will rise again after New Year's Day, otherwise we won't have any profit this year. Everything seems to go wrong, and often I have wished we were still in our old homeland, although I have it better here. If it only were not so terribly far so that we could get together at least once a year. I would have so much to tell and would so much like to see your darling little boys, dear Sister. When I look at Ernst's picture again and again, I feel

39

terribly homesick. I wish to see him face to face and his dear parents and brothers and sisters. You wrote in your last letter that you would enclose some hair of dear Ernst's. Did you forget it? I looked it over and over and could not find it. Please, send me some and also of Fritz's. Here is some of little Rudolf's.[5] Thank God he is always well and such a dear little boy. Fred and Hans have gone to school since the beginning of October. They like it. They leave at nine o'clock and have an hour break at noon. Teachers and pupils take their lunches with them, so I have to make many sandwiches and cookies. In the evening, dear Rudolf runs to meet them when he sees them and it is not too cold. We have already had cold days; then Grandfather's coats are very handy. Both have felt boots, and in milder weather they wear leather boots. The weather has been the coldest since New Year's Day, and we need heat day and night. Fortunately, we have plenty of fuel, much wood and two huge heaps of corn cobs. This year there aren't as many since most farmers shell the corn in the spring. Let's hope next year we have a better harvest.

Brother Fritz wrote that you moved into a new cheese factory. Good luck for you in it. Do you like your new place? It is a pity that you are so far away from Ernst. Is their new house finished, and do they live in it already? They also had a sad blow. How does Emma like Goldbach? Next time, do write much news to me. I would like to hear from Father and Mother. Brother Fritz writes they were both with you. Give them my greetings and tell them to always keep the stove nicely warm, and if time seems long to them, they should write me a long letter! Greetings and thanks also to my brother. If or when we have our pictures taken, I don't know when, we would send them to you. We would have done it if it had been a better year. So don't be angry with us. When you see my sister-in-law in Goldbach,[6] tell her that Marianne will soon be a grandmother. I will soon write to Elisabeth in Jegenstorfand also my cousin Rosetti Bosch-Marti. Are you always well, especially you, Anna? I'll hope for the best. Your little one will be nine months old when you get my letter. Yes, the time goes fast, and we are now already almost two years away from home; and in eight years, if God keeps us well, we'll come to Switzerland again, if not before.

For the new year which will soon be here, I wish you God's blessings, contentment and health. I hope you'll remember us with love as we do you. Fritz and the children send a thousand greetings.
Your Sister and Sister-in-law
Louise Ritter

[1]Luebke, *Immigrants and Politics,* p. 38.
[2]Ibid.
[3]The years 1876-1892 are described as a wet period with one very dry year (1890). But the

years 1893-1901 are recorded as a dry period with one rather wet year. Olson, *History of Nebraska*, p. 13. The recorded precipitation at Oakdale, about six miles from their farm, was 11.48. Olson gives 13.54 for the state average. The highest temperature recorded was 110 degrees in July of that year. Leach, *A History of Antelope County*, pp. 260-261. Everett Dick states, "But to the struggling pioneer in the semi-arid part of the state who had not accumulated resources . . . 1894 was beyond realistic optimism." Dick, *Conquering the Great American Desert*, p. 334.

[4]She kept accurate record. Olson records 49 and 50¢ for wheat.

[5]The curl is still attached to the letter.

[6]Anna Ritter Schupback – one of Fritz's sisters who never left Switzerland.

SUMMARY OF 1895

There are no letters from Louise during 1895. Perhaps the letters were destroyed, or maybe she could not bring herself to write and describe the conditions. Even though the year of 1895 had more rainfall, recovery was extremely slow. Many people left the plains, never to return.[1] For those who remained it was no longer a question of making money, but of survival. It was estimated that 15,000 farm families were destitute. To help the people, appropriations from the state treasury included $50,000 for food and clothing and $200,000 to buy seed and feed for their teams so destitute farmers would be able to put in a crop for 1895.[2]

Antelope County, the home of the Ritters, was one of those areas receiving aid. In February, the *Oakdale Sentinel* included this relief notice: "There will be a distribution of relief supplies at Neligh, Thursday and Friday of next week, Feb. 7th and 8th. Flour and meal will be given out, also coal should be in sufficient quantity to be received by that time."[3] The same notice was repeated the following week. Other relief agencies were active; sometimes the results were different than expected. In March the *Oakdale Sentinel* included this item:

The *Tilden Citizen* would have its readers believe that there were many destitute families in Oakdale. It says: "The Methodist relief committee distributed supplies to 40 destitute families in Oakdale last Saturday." You are wrong, Mr. Citizen ... only six families of Oakdale received any of these supplies.[4]

The rivalry between the towns might give a modern reader a laugh or two, but the problems were grim as the summary of the amount of relief supplies indicates. Between November 1, 1894, to March 1, 1895, the following supplies were sent from Missouri to Antelope County: "Flour, 241,800 lbs., 5,036 sacks at 90¢, $4,532.40; corn meal, 125,900 lbs., at $1 per cwt., $1,259; bacon, 3,000 lbs., at 10¢ per lb., $300; coal, 360,000 lbs., 180 tons, at $4.50 per ton, $810; Total, $6,901.40."[5] In later years Fritz would comment that it was good the help had been available, but it had not been necessary for them to use it.

Since the rainfall had increased from 11.48 to 23.85, the Ritters had the promise of a good crop for the first time since they had arrived in Nebraska. About harvest time, a hail storm struck their grain. It went through the field to the fence line, and then returned to destroy what remained. The neighbor's crop was untouched.[6] The *Oakdale Sentinel* describes a storm on Saturday, August 10, 1895.

As near as we can ascertain, a straight line drawn through the northwest corner of Neligh township ... to Tilden will approximately give the center of last Saturday's hail storm. The farmers situated on or near this line are the heaviest losers, some of them more than others, depending entirely upon the freaks of the storm.

The appearance of the storm must have been foreboding: "But as it approached signs of hail were plainly apparent in its appearance . . . the dark, heavy clouds of the main body were of a decidedly greenish hue when not lit up by the almost continuous blaze of lightning." In Tilden all window glass exposed to the storm was smashed. "Twenty-four telegraph poles were blown down near Tilden – eleven at Tilden and thirteen about one mile west of Tilden . . . ." Further comments on the storm stated that "throughout the hail strip corn was damaged 10 to 50 percent. But the copious rainfall (1.16 inches at Oakdale) that accompanied the storm will do much to offset this damage."[7] This would have offered little comfort to the Ritters or the others who lost their crop.

The disappointments and financial insecurity would have been enough to keep Louise from writing. Louise had an additional concern; she was pregnant with her fifth child, who was born March 10, 1896.

A neighbor of theirs during those early years reported that whenever he went by the place there was always a Ritter working in the fields. They were the first in and the last to leave the fields. Maybe Jules Sandoz was not so far wrong when he recruited German Swiss for his settlement. "Although he never told Mary so, it was because she was such a hard worker, made all the other women he knew seem lazy, impractical, and irresponsible, that Jules turned his settling activities toward Germans and German Swiss."[8] He was satisfied with them when they arrived. "The Germans and the German Swiss didn't visit as much as the French, but they made good settlers. They carried lanterns until late at night, complained of the wind, the cold, and the drouth, and prospered well enough."[9] Louise and Fritz had to wait a few more years for their prosperity.

[1]Lawson, Dewey, and Neild, *Climatic Atlas of Nebraska,* p. 54.
[2]Sheldon, I, p. 756.
[3]*Oakdale Sentinel,* 2 February 1895, p. 1.
[4]*Oakdale Sentinel,* 2 March 1895, p. 1.
[5]"Relief Report," *Oakdale Sentinel,* 27 July 1895, p. 8.
[6]Interview, Ernest Ritter, December 1978.
[7]*Oakdale Sentinel,* 17 August 1895, p. 1.
[8]Mari Sandoz, *Old Jules* (Lincoln, Nebraska: University of Nebraska Press, 1962), p. 221.
[9]Ibid., p. 223.

INTRODUCTORY NOTE
For Letter of October 25, 1896

Many of the problems described in this letter have been presented in fiction. Louise reported the birth of the new child in March, but there was regret that those in the homeland could not see the child and rejoice with them.[1] Certainly, Louise reflected none of the terror of Rölvaag's Beret who questioned bringing a new child into this wilderness, but she must have wondered how his and her other sons' futures would be shaped by the Nebraska environment. The family had just seen their joy in a good crop quickly destroyed by a cholera epidemic which killed their hogs. Sophus Winther in *Take All to Nebraska* gives several scenes describing the economic impact of the death of livestock to a struggling farmer.

Oscar Handlin provides an excellent parallel to help us understand the situation of the immigrant.

> Among the themes upon which the process of migration throws light is one that has been particularly important in the shaping of modern society. The immigrants experienced in an extreme form what other modern men have felt – the consequences of the breakdown of traditional communal life. This decisive development, about which little is yet known has significantly influenced American character. One need not feel any sense of nostalgia for the old community to recognize its importance and also the importance of its passing.[2]

Just as there is no going back for us, there was no return for them. They tried to reconstruct the old communities, but the immigrants in the United States could not restore the community destroyed by migration.

Tilden, October 25, 1896

Dear Parents,

My answer to your dear, last letter comes late. Please excuse me. I am so glad that you were successful in selling your cheeses at all three places, but I am also afraid you don't make enough profit since you have to pay so much for the milk. But I regret that you, dear Parents, had to find such people. It is especially bad for Father with his health problem. It is like that – there are bad people everywhere. I hope that it is better now, and I suppose in the spring you will discontinue your cheese making.

We are having an exceptionally good year – lots of wheat, hay, corn – we hardly know where to put it all.[3] We have had enough rain, but not rainy weather. Most of the rain has come at night. Today it is very hot. The hay would easily dry in one day. At night we have considerable frost. For three weeks now, everybody has been busy with the corn harvest. Unfortunately,

45

in spite of this rich blessing from heaven, we have to tell you a bad "however." We heard already in early summer that there was some cholera among the hogs. Then for a while all was quiet again until they said that almost all hogs were dying in Tilden. At the end of August it started again in our neighborhood, and we were glad to be able to sell the big healthy hogs, thirty-six of them. Ten large ones died, then the little ones got sick. It was terrible to watch. We had 130 and only seven are left. The old pigs had to be taken away thin and light in weight. Usually, when we needed some money, we sold some hogs.[4] Now the old ones are gone and the little ones are dead. This almost only source of money is gone.

November 2. I must also say here that a misfortune hardly comes alone. On Sunday evening of October 18 when Fritz and I were reading the newspaper in the dining room, Fred came and called out that our haystacks were on fire. Oh, how frightened we were! The flames were already high, and although there was a strong south wind and the fire was on the north side, soon all six haystacks and the horse barn were in full flames. Soon help came from all sides. If we had had a north wind like the one on the next day, we would most likely have lost everything – the two barns full of grain, one built only last summer, the stables, etc. The house is further away so it was safe.[5] Fritz burnt his right hand and face quite badly. His face will soon be all right again, but it will take longer with his hand. You may ask, how did the fire happen? The answer is a very, very sad one. Hans[6] had made a little fire under a haystack and so caused the misfortune. We still have about the same amount of hay in another place as we have lost. If we had not been at home, we would have also lost our four horses which were in the barns. May God preserve you from such misfortune and fright.

Sorry not to have written to Anna and Emma, but I hope to do it soon. Emma sent me that lovely, woolen blanket for my darling,[7] and you sent me in September the stockings and fur slippers which I enjoyed so much. Many thanks.

Oh, if only we were still close to you! Of course, there also is hardship in our dear Switzerland.[8] I read of it in your letters and in the newspapers, but it seems to hurt doubly in a foreign land because we still feel homesick. If you only would move to us in the spring, you could have a marvelous life here. You could have a nice house and could eat well, and you could loan your money with high interest, eight percent. I won't have much luck in enticing you to come here, but how I would love it!

Tomorrow will be the great battle in America; the election of the President and the great money question. May all turn out well. Improvement is really needed; an increase in commerce and trade would cause farm prices to rise.[9]

At present we fatten twenty-three cattle, and soon after we will have another car load. We have now fifty-one head of cattle. With this fattening process, we could have forty pigs without giving them anything but water. Of course, the water would not fatten them, but they would eat what the cows leave.[10] The hog disease is not yet over, and there is some loss of cattle. Uli's for instance had to slaughter three or four cattle in one week.

Hoping that this letter reaches you in good health, and thousand greetings from Fritz, Louise and the children.
Write soon again.

[1]When a new baby is born in a Swiss village it is customary for relatives, neighbors, and acquaintances to visit. They bring gifts, and the mother takes them to the baby's room to admire the baby, his crib blanket, and other furnishings. The mother often gives gift chocolates or cookies to her guests. Weinberg, *Peasant Wisdom,* p. 60.

[2]Oscar Handlin, "Immigration in American Life, a Reappraisal" in *Immigration and American History,* p. 12.

[3]The Nebraska crop of 1895 produced a surplus, "but prices continued to fall, and the accumultion of past due debts and taxes ate up the crop. Dec. 1, 1895 average farm prices of grain and livestock were the lowest up to that date in the record of our state." The following prices were offered per bushel: Wheat, 40¢; Corn, 18¢; Oats, 14¢. For stock milk cows the price per head was $16.85; other cattle, $13.68. The peak of the depression was in 1896. Sheldon, *Nebraska,* I, pp. 759, 768.

[4]Hogs sold for $4.90 a head. Sheldon, I, p. 759.

[5]The Tilden and Oakdale papers included no reports of the fire.

[6]Hans was eight years old.

[7]Her "darling" is the son William, born that March.

[8]Switzerland was becoming more industrialized and from 1893 to 1895 was in a tariff war with France. Because Switzerland must export, protective tariffs actually damage the economy. Martin, *Switzerland,* p. 252.

[9]This election was at the time of the Populists, William Jennings Bryan, and the issue of free silver. McKinley was elected. Bryan's 6,468,000 ballots in 1896 were more than any Democrat would get again for twenty years. This was the last protest of the old agrarian order against industrialism. For a dozen years Populists tried to keep the party, but the Populist revolt collapsed because the Democrats had appropriated the issues and because most of their cause of discontent was removed by a revival of general prosperity. Shannon, *The Farmer's Last Frontier,* pp. 322-326.

It is not valid to assume that the overwhelming majority of Nebraska farmers did join the movement. The Ritters could not vote in the election, but they must have found American politics strange. The Swiss constitutional government has no single man at the head of any of the executive branches. The President is merely chairman. The cabinet members are elected, and there must be a coalition cabinet representing principal parties. They were accustomed to a preoccupation with one's canton and a lukewarm interest in federal government. Herold, *The Swiss Without Halos,* pp. 228-229.

Why did they not enter into the Populist movement since they were suffering as many other farmers? The Populist movement was a revolt. It would take time for them to understand what they were revolting against. One reason was their background of conservatism. They had no history of revolt against fuedalism; the origin of the Swiss nation is to be found where feudalism had never existed. The Swiss had fought to maintain conditions as they were. Traditionally Swiss have accepted the direct challenge of nature in pursuit of a livelihood. Here, the Ritters were not dealing with the Alps, but were still confronting nature. Also, as a poor country, Switzerland survived and prospered not by dreams but by realism and transforming ideas into cash. For hundreds of years the limitations under which the Swiss had labored developed frugality and thrift to learn to do what you can with what you have. The Ritters did not believe in a movement but in themselves. Herold, pp. 22, 149, 155, 207-208.

The vote in Antelope County in the 1896 election was divided as follows: Republicans, 989; Democrats, 20, Democratic-Populists, 1,234; National, 7; Prohibition, 28. the vote in Burnett Township where the Ritters lived was as follows: Republicans, 66; Democrats, 2; Democratic-Populists, 56; none for the last two parties. The people living in their area were more conservative than the rest of the county. "Official Canvass of the Vote of Antelope County, Nov. 3, 1896," *Neligh Advocate,* 20 November 1896, p. 1.

[10]In Switzerland it was customary to have a few pigs with the cattle in the stables. With almost no work there would be an extra source of food or income. Weinberg, p. 21.

Immigrants often idealized home conditions but at the same time wished to gain recognition in the homeland, especially if they planned to return. But the immigrant was living in the New World, so he also wished to improve his status in the eyes of those among whom he was now living. Because he felt alien to American life, he attempted to create a situation in which he could participate.[1] To a certain extent, Louise illustrates the generalization. A part of her was involved in the life across the ocean; she hoped to return. But she was concerned for the education of her sons, and she wanted a prosperous and secure future in Nebraska.

This letter was written in the spring of 1897. Rainfall was adequate, 25.17,[2] so crops were raised in 1897, but prices were low. Wheat brought 55¢, oats 7¢, and shelled corn 9¢ a bushel.[3] The situation during the winter had been so bad that many people in Elgin, a neighboring town, burned corn as fuel. The paper reported that in the yards of all the residences were great piles of corn being used as fuel since it was much cheaper than coal.[4] Just a month before this letter cows sold for $3.00 per hundredweight, hogs for $3.40, and eggs for 8¢ a dozen.[5] The same paper indicated prices of dress goods for 15¢ a yard and shoes for $1.25. There seemed to be no way to win.

Tilden, April 15, 1897

Much Beloved Ones,

As so often, my answer unfortunately comes very late. I meant to write to you immediately after I had written to Emma, so there was nothing for you in that letter, not even a greeting – please forgive me. On New Year's Day we received a calendar from Konig,[6] and a few days afterwards your letters.

The new year began with rain, then immediately hard frost. On January 2, a heavy snow storm started which lasted two days and nights. It was a terrible storm with more wind than we had ever seen before. The newspapers and also our friends said that it was the most violent snow storm since twenty years ago.[7] It was not especially cold, but there was so much snow which had drifted to high heaps that we were afraid the cattle would suffocate. In some places many died. The snow had to be shoveled to get to the cattle. In deep places the drifts are not yet melted. As sunshine follows rain, so also often after a snow storm. We had never had as much snow as in this winter. In January and February we had many warm and sunny days, but Mr. Winter played his tricks in March and April, so that the sowing had to be started very late. We sowed our oats and wheat last week – before Palm Sunday.[8] In the lower regions it will be much later, if it is not too late altogether.

We had a lot of rain this spring. In the Mississippi Valley, thousands are without shelter because of floods. You may read about it in your Emmental paper. Uli's don't get it anymore since the new year, so we cannot get much news from our homeland.

How is Emma? I wonder what the stork brought them, and if all are well.[9] Anna will also have her hands full with the little ones.[10] If they can only be in good health. I have not heard a word yet if you are buying your milk still in the same three places or if there have been changes. It seems to me that you worked hard enough in your younger days so that you ought to have quiet and pleasant days now. Brother Fritz has cost a lot of money. What is he doing now? He ought to be old enough to support himself.[11] Pardon me if I interfere, but I am his sister and unfortunately know about the trouble.

Is Aunt Mary still in Heimenhausen and Aunt Julie in Messen? I heard from the former one that Marie from Russia[12] visited Switzerland for three months. Did she often visit you? I hope so. Oh, if only I could come to you soon with my sweet Willie and darling Rudolf – how you would enjoy them. Yes, Grandfather and Grandmother, Rudolf asked me to tell you that you should come to us. He wants to show you all we have. Do come and all brothers and sisters. There is much room here, and my children would enjoy so much visiting people whom they love.

I resent the school so much. Fred could know so much if he had been able to go to school. They had only three months of school before the new year began, and will have only five or six months altogether. Fritz wants to say something about it at the next school meeting.[13]

We had a bad time losing all those hogs. We have only six little ones left, and they look bad enough. The epidemic is not yet over. In some places it has come a second time.

I realize you would like to have a picture of us, but goodness knows when that will be.

Dear Father, you asked last fall if one can buy Swiss cheese here. I am not sure, but I doubt it except in large cities. Yes, if you would send us one that would be delightful. The children love it. We get some sometimes from Uli. I meant to write for the balsam recipe for a long time. The balsam that Elisabeth[14] brought me was good for me. Could you send me some as a "sample without value." Dear Father, if you would write to us and tell us how to tan hides that would be of great service. When you see Elisabeth, tell her that our Willie is taller than Gottfried's Lina.[15] He is also heavier, but cannot yet walk because he is too heavy. He is a darling and his three brothers love him.

I'll write soon to Anna. My best greetings to all my brothers and sisters and their families. I would like to encourage brother to be very diligent so

that he can soon do something useful.
With our greeting to you all. I am always your
Louise Ritter

[1]Bernard, *Americanization Studies,* p. 142.
[2]Leach, *A History of Antelope County,* p. 260.
[3]*Tilden Citizen,* 20 March 1897, p. 3.
[4]*Tilden Citizen,* 9 January 1897, p. 1.
[5]*Tilden Citizen,* 20 March 1897, p. 3.
[6]Her sister Emma had married Konig.
[7]She might have exaggerated the storm slightly, but the account in the paper supports her statement that the storm was severe. It does not indicate the death of cattle as she does. "This country experienced the most severe blizzard for six years past, last Sunday and Monday. A heavy gale started on Sunday morning and was accompanied by a heavy fall of snow which held its own with the wind and continued to fall until Monday evening. The result is that the town and country is full of immense drifts ranging from a few inches to 15 feet in height.... No teams came in town from the country until quite late on Tuesday, the first to arrive having experienced considerable difficulty in making their way through the immense drifts.... We have heard of no loss of life or stock during the storm for which the people have just cause to be thankful." *Tilden Citizen,* 9 January 1897, p. 3.
[8]There was no significance in planting by Palm Sunday. It merely served as a way of indicating time. They did not plant according to any such folklore. Interview, Ernest Ritter, February 1979.
[9]Emma's child was girl, Anna, the first of her four children.
[10]Her sister Anna had five children now.
[11]At the time of this letter, her brother was twenty-five years old. He was the youngest of the four and nine years younger than Louise. He was educated and became a teacher. There is no record as to what the "trouble" was.
[12]In the years from 1821 to 1846 families from Switzerland were a small part of the emigration from Germany to Russia. There were Swiss in colonies established in Schabo, Volga, Crimea, and South Caucasus. In the Volga region there were nine colonies named after Swiss cantons – Unterwalden, Zug, Lucerne, Glarus, Basel, Berne (soon dissolved), Zurich, Solothurn, and Schaffhausen. The groups included both Catholics and Protestants. Karl Stumpp, *The Emigration from Germany to Russia in the Years 1763 to 1862* (Lincoln, Nebraska: American Historical Society of Germans from Russia, 1973), pp. 20, 22, 87, 99. No information is available on whether Marie from Russia was a member of one of these groups.
[13]"The first school in Burnett Township was started in 1872 in a log building. In 1880, the pupils were moved to a frame building.... The school board ... probably conducted the business meeting in Swiss as many of the settlers there were from Switzerland. The school term was short, 160 days, and attendance poor." *History of Antelope County 1883-1973,* p. 21.
   According to the 1900 census, Grant was the only township in Antelope county other than Burnett which had settlers from Switzerland. Grant had three who came over in 1873 and 1882. Burnett, where the Ritters lived, had twenty-seven listed. Three had come over early, in 1843, 1868, and 1875. The rest had arrived between the years of 1890 to 1894. United States Census Office, *Twelfth Census of the United States: 1900 Population,* I, Nebraska, Antelope county microfilm.
[14]Elisabeth was one of Fritz's older sisters who came to the United States but later returned to Switzerland.
[15]Granddaughter of Fritz's sister Marianne.

INTRODUCTORY NOTE
For Letters of September 4, December 11, 1898, and February 26, 1899

George Santayana said that in North America all of the immigrants, with the exception of the Negroes, were voluntary exiles and that the American accordingly was the most adventurous or the descendant of the most adventurous of the Europeans.[1] Louise reflected confidence and optimism in the letters of 1898 and 1899. The sense of adventure and willingness to experiment are found in the letters and her statements about Fritz. The immigrant's enthusiasm for the future was seen in his willingness to listen to new opinions and try new ways because others were adopting them. Fritz bought the new machinery, and Louise learned to cope with Yankee eating habits.

Unfortunately, little information has been preserved relating to the domestic work of women on the farm before 1900. Apparently farm women in the late 1800s were no more prone to insanity than their city sisters. They were too busy to bother much with their solitude, and their drudgery was a varied sort. Their amusements were few and rare, but when they came they could enjoy them because of their novelty.[2] Louise wrote little about amusements other than Christmas and New Year's Day. She told about her work with no self-pity. At least they were beginning to prosper now.

Tilden, September 4, 1898

Much Beloved Parents,

It is high time to tell you a bit about us again. In your last letter you apologized about your long wait with writing. I was not cross about it, although I would like to hear from you much oftener. I have to ask for your pardon, too. Summer with its many activities, and often with suffocating heat (especially last week with the south wind singing night and day) approaches its end. Our wheat has been in shocks for a long time and is waiting to be threshed. We cut and shocked our ninety acres of wheat without outside help in two weeks. A good harvest machine is well worth its price.[3]

The hay cutting is also finished. Here one cuts the hay after the harvest. Up to the harvest there is always work to do in the corn fields, and if the hay were cut early, it would not keep. Emma wrote me that you had such unfavorable weather for drying your hay.[4] There is no problem for that here. The hay is cut by machines, raked into heaps with the horse rake, and in the same day it is as dry as you wish.

In the spring we had a lot of rain, early summer was dry, and it was high time when in early and middle July heavy downpours occurred. Otherwise

53

our corn would have been lost. But now the corn fields are a real joy; the ears as long as a forearm. Last week we shelled 900 bushels of last year's corn ----

[Letter is incomplete]

Happy New Year 1899
Tilden, December 11, 1898

My Dear Ones,

It is always the same old story with my writing early; it always gets so long. When you receive this letter, it will be Christmas or even later. It would be so nice if I could once more in my life celebrate Christmas with my parents or brothers and sisters in my homeland. There, a lighted tree will give your children much joy. My children have not had a Christmas tree; pine trees do not grow here. Once in a while one sees a yellow sick little pine tree, but the ground is not suited for them. In our yard are five cedar trees, but they are not so beautifully green in winter as our pines and firs.

I wish you, dear Sister, and your family a Merry Christmas and a Happy New Year. God's blessings on your work and may He protect you from illness and other miseries. I would like to hear about your health, but I hope for the best. I don't know anything of your cheese trade and of Iffwyl. In my last letter to Emma I forgot to ask – may she forgive me. Dear Anna, please give Sister Emma many thanks for the house guests of last fall. Emma also asked about the war,[5] and I forgot all about it until the letter was closed. We didn't feel much of the war, saw less, and I nothing at all. We saw a few passenger trains with military come through. Many young men feared they would be drafted when the rumor was that Germany would help Spain.[6] Now, thank God, we have peace again. The war expense was put on sugar, tea, coffee, and beer, I think. Also the postage went up. Farm products yielded a good price. So we were not damaged by the war, but we are glad that there is peace now. There is quite a lot in the papers these days which throws a strange light on high military dignitaries.[7]

By next Sunday, December 18, we will have our corn crop picked, unless very bad weather interferes. We are satisfied with it – we have a lot of corn and for two months we have been feeding the cattle corn. At present we have ninety-five. We haven't lost any through the summer and fall, although we were afraid of sickness in the fall. We also have seventy hogs, over fifty chickens but no eggs. The hens are on strike. I killed the roosters earlier for us to eat. Once in a while a wolf[8] comes; in one night he killed thirteen chickens. In the middle of September, we threshed with a steam thresher and finished it all in one and a half days. Last year and this year I did all the cooking myself, since by now I know a bit of the Yankee's favorites. They like a lot of sugar in baking and coffee. We ourselves don't like sugar too well. Sometimes something sweet is nice, but vegetables, meat and potatoes are better for us!

We have already had a few very cold days. I cannot describe how the cold winds can blow. It is as if it would tear your face. Fritz said recently that we could be much afraid of the American winter if we were not now familiar with it. But with many mild days we can thaw again. We now have three school boys. Dear Rudolf marches along with his older brothers. He did not like it a bit that he had to stay at home last week because of the cold weather.

Saturday, December 17. My letter is not yet finished and will be too late for Christmas, but perhaps in time for New Year's Day. Again a happy and blessed New Year, my dear ones, to all, the dear parents, Emma and the family in Iffwyl and also Brother Fritz. Are they all well and will they soon write to me?

I am very glad that the corn harvest is over now. Fritz has a bad hand and would not be able to help. I think it is a boil; he also had two on his neck and Hans has one on his foot. Darling Willie has a sore throat. So we have little troubles, but on the whole we are all right. How are our aunts in Messen; is Aunt Mary always sick? I think often of Cousin Marie.

I have to close now. Best greetings to all; a kiss to your little one, dear Anna.

Always yours,
Louise Ritter

Tilden, February 26, 1899

My Very Dear Parents,

I want to shake hands with you again and look into your eyes and tell you of our experiences in the foreign land personally. That would be so much better than writing letters, don't you agree? I hope so very much that my sister-in-law and I can take a trip to Switzerland – how I am longing for it. We would prefer that her son Gottfried could accompany us, for without manly protection I would hardly risk it. You understand that Fritz cannot get away from here. I would love to take my darling Willie with me.

How did you fare this winter? We are still in the midst of it. May you both be well. How do you like Iffwyl? I do hope you like it there. Emma is close to you.

Rosetti in Jegenstorf has owed me a letter for three years. Is she still alive? I often think of Uli's in Utzinstorf. They could have a better home here in Nebraska and would not have to work so hard. We now have 480 acres of our own land and 110 head of cattle.[9] There is not much work needed for them in the summer because they are in the fields the whole day. We also have nine horses, over sixty hogs, and fifty chickens.

The two older boys, Fred and Hans, are tall for their age and can help. Last year we had 140 acres of corn and 90 of wheat and oats. This year we have 140 acres more which were rented last year. Wheat is sown in the spring.[10] The crops were excellent the last three years and yielded good prices. In our area every healthy farmer earned $700. We are thinking of building a nice brick cellar[11] and a large kitchen this summer. They are both much needed.

We have to take some pictures this spring. Little Willie wears pants now. On March 10 he will be three years old. How are Sister-in-law Anna and family? Your last letter arrived the same day Fritz mailed a letter to Anna, so I hope for more news from you soon. Please share this letter with her and greetings to all, also to the aunts in Messen and the relatives who remember us. Do Kunzs in Mulchi ask about us? I would like to write to them if I could expect an answer.

Please, write Box not Bax on the envelope. Do write soon again. Tell me also about Brother Fritz – he never writes. Fritz is taking some oats to Tilden and will mail my letter. Greetings from him, and he thinks he might visit you one day too! God knows when! The best from me and the children to you all.

Always yours,

Louise Ritter

Tell me also about the milk and cheese business.

[1] John T. Flanagan, "the Immigrant in Western Fiction," in *Immigration and American History*, p. 86.

[2] Shannon, *The Farmer's Last Frontier*, p. 367.

[3] See October 22, 1893, note 4, for information on the improvement of the binder.

[4] The drying racks for hay are a common sight in Europe.

[5] Spanish-American.

[6] Europe came near to forming a monarchial front against the United States; Emperor William II proposed it as early as September 1897. He had hoped to purchase the Philippines from Spain and put down the insurrection. Admiral von Diederichs attempted to defy Dewey's blockade of Manila and paraded his ships past the American squadron with guns trained on them. A British naval squadron leader interposed his ships between the Americans and the Germans. Samuel Eliot Morison, *The Oxford History of the American People* (New York: Oxford University Press, 1965), pp. 802, 805.

[7] It is difficult to know what she is referring to in this comment. There were charges of imperialism after the war began. Bryan is reported going to McKinley and stating that Nebraska volunteers felt they should be mustered out because the issues of the war changed. "They volunteered to break the yoke of Spain in Cuba, and for nothing else. They did not volunteer to attempt the subjugation of other peoples, or establish United States sovereignty elsewhere." Margaret Leech, *In the Days of McKinley* (New York: Harper and Brothers, 1959), p. 338.

[8] It is more likely that the animal would be coyote. Wolves were plentiful on the plains, and "that smaller wolf-like creature, the coyote, is also common to grassland." Durward L. Allen, *The Life of Prairies and Plains* (New York: McGraw-Hill Book Co., 1967), p. 96.

[9]In 1900, the average size of a farm in Nebraska was 246.1 acres. In Antelope County the average size was 269.8, with 168 farms over 500 acres, 470 farms between 260 to 500 acres, 1,097 farms under 260 acres. United States Census Office, *Twelfth Census of the United States: 1900, Agriculture,* I, p. 102. The Ritters were prospering.

[10]In Antelope County "the first cultivated crops consisted of sod corn and garden vegetables, followed by corn, oats, and wheat as conditions became more stable. Corn has always been the leading grain crop. Wheat was grown chiefly for sale. Most of the wheat was of the spring varieties." Even in 1921 spring wheat was planted in one-fourth of the total acreage. F.A. Hayes, et al, *Soil Survey of Antelope County, Nebraska* (Washington: U.S. Dept. of Agriculture, 1924), pp. 762, 764.

[11]The cellar was to be under the house; the soil was too sandy for digging caves.

Louise's brother Fritz

Left to right: Rudolf, Fritz, Fred (back), Willie (front), Louise, Hans.

INTRODUCTORY NOTE
For letter of July 8, 1900

The new century brought an improved economic situation to Nebraska and to the Ritter family. The tone of this letter reflects this improvement. Between 1900 and 1910, per acre value of land and buildings rose about 100 percent and then climbed another 90 percent by 1920. In Nebraska and Kansas land values increased 157 and 177 percent respectively.[1] This prosperity was partially the result of improved weather. The drought of 1893-1895 was followed by a thirty-five year period of normal to near normal precipitation.[2] Not all crops were uniformly good every year, but no part of the state suffered from prolonged drought or repeated destruction by insect pests.[3] Rainfall amounts for their area from 1900 through 1905 ranged from 26.26 to 36.07 inches, a definite improvement from the 1894 amount of only 11.48.[4] The decades of industrial depression had reduced purchasing power and contributed to low prices. After 1900 the rate of physical expansion in agriculture was much slower than it had been during the previous thirty years. After 1900 only about four million acres of land were added to American farms annually, compared to around fifteen million acres before that date. This meant that there was a leveling off of production, or at most only a modest increase. While production remained relatively steady, prices rose sharply. Wheat brought 62¢ a bushel at the farm in 1900, but had risen to 90¢ by 1910, and to 43¢ by 1916 under the impact of war in Europe. By 1918 it reached more than $2 a bushel and would have gone much higher if it had not been for government controls.[5] Prices received for their produce increased, but more importantly the prices for items that had to be bought did not rise proportionately. The 1909 value of ten leading farm crops rose 72 percent and many things farmers had to buy increased 12 percent. Using 1899 as an index of 100, the value of farm products rose to 189 during the next ten years.[6]

Prosperity enabled the farmer to add to and improve his equipment. New barns made it easier to care for livestock. Riding implements such as the cultivator came into general use. The blow stacker, manure spreader, horse fork, and other laborsaving equipment took a great deal of the drudgery out of farm life, and larger machinery reduced the hours of labor.[7]

What was available for the farmer's wife? Though some farm homes could boast an oil stove, carpet sweeper, sinks, running water, the farmer's wife generally had to do much of her work in the same old way. She still spent long hours over the kitchen range preparing food for the family and hired help.[8] Louise's work ranged from preserving fruits, cheese making, to helping in the field. What almost destroyed her was not the work but the series of tragedies she had to endure this decade.

59

Beloved Parents,

I am ashamed and apologize that I let you write twice before answering you. Fritz scolded me too. One day after the other passes in such a hurry that we are almost breathless.

Much has happened here in that time and with you, too, as I learn from your letters. Both of you seem to be in good health now, compared to the winter. I am so happy for this good news. I was sick last winter also. From the beginning of December to the middle of January, I had an ear ache that sometimes was so bad that I thought I would lose my mind. I hesitated going to the doctor, but he helped me quickly. He said my ear drums were torn and that he had the same trouble. When we had to call him for Willie on March 10, he asked me about my ear, and I told him that it had been all right for a long time. His ear was not good but still painful. In five weeks he was dead. We could hardly believe it. He had to suffer much and had painful operations to take bones out behind his ear. I mention it because this man was a real humanitarian whose profession meant all to him; he was always ready to help. He was only thirty-nine years old. His funeral was on Easter Monday, and all who knew him mourned for him.[9] Tilden now has four doctors, one a German one.[10]

So, Sister-in-law Anna is now in Zeeland.[11] I can imagine that it was hard for her to get used to it. I do hope they will be happy there. I'll write them soon – give them my greetings. I expect an answer from Brother Fritz soon and a picture of his wife. Why doesn't Emma write to us? She is very busy, I suppose. I do hope that her husband, Fritz, is good to her. Your strawberries are all eaten now I suppose, so are our mulberries and raspberries. Soon there will be cherries, plums, and grapes. They all grow wild and make wonderful jellies and a strong wine. Our fields are our pride and joy. Already tomorrow we'll begin to harvest our oats. I wish you could see our wheat fields. We have fifty acres of wheat, seventy of oats – an early and a later kind. The cutting is done by machinery. Fred rides in front of it with two horses. Three weeks ago we had another colt, Willie's greatest joy.

Sunday, July 15. We began harvesting last Tuesday and could have been through if it had not stormed and rained. We had wheat and oats this year that were very good, but much will be lost because it is getting too ripe. The rain was very good for the corn. This week we had bad days with hot winds which were hard on people, animals, and plants. Ten days ago, Fritz took a second load of cattle to Omaha, twenty-three head. Their average weight was 1055 pounds. The same day there were 3,453 cattle at the market, 8,065 hogs, 702 sheep, and 500 horses. There is a market every day except Sundays and holidays. Often they have much more at the market. In the beginning of June, Fritz went with twenty head of cattle to Omaha. This year we

60

also have fine hogs, and now we still have from forty-five to fifty. We don't know how many suckling pigs we have, about eighty. I had over one hundred chickens; I lost some and sold nine roosters at 15¢ each. That was for a small size. Butter sells at 12¢ a pound and eggs 7¢ a dozen. Imagine, dear Parents, I am now also making cheese.[12] I have already sold forty pieces. We all like the cheese, but I would like to have some rennet in powder form. Would it be possible, dear Father, to send me a small box wrapped in a new cheese cloth with the word "Sample" on it? I would be so glad and thank you already in advance. My cheese cloth is all torn.

I have to finish my letter now. Tomorrow I am going to town and can take it to the Post Office. We need twine for the binder. Yesterday, we could cut only in the afternoon; today we can cut the whole day. There are many bundles. I helped this afternoon, too. I shocked more than a hundred bundles. Yes, that binder is a machine. I wish you could see it work. Do come, dear Parents; Fritz will give you some land where you can build a nice little house, and you can have a cow and a horse and lots of chickens.

With greetings from us all to all.

Louise Ritter.

[1]Gilbert C. Fite, *American Agriculture and Farm Policy Since 1900* (New York: The Macmillan Co., 1964), p. 6.

[2]Lawson, Dewey, and Neild, *Climatic Atlas of Nebraska,* p. 55.

[3]Olson, *History of Nebraska,* p. 260.

[4]Ibid.

[5]Fite, p. 5.

[6]Ibid., p. 6.

[7]Olson, p. 261.

[8]Ibid.

[9]"Dr. Scofield of Tilden died last Saturday in a hospital in Omaha where he went for treatment. An operation was performed, from which he died naturally. Cerebramenigitis is given as the cause of death." *Oakdale Sentinel,* 21 April 1900, p. 1.

[10]"It appears that immigrant institutions operative in the rural and small town environment were fairly successful in easing the process whereby the newcomer was assimilated, mostly, perhaps by slowing it down. Small town merchants hired bilingual clerks; professional people who could speak German advertised the fact; . . . ." Luebke, *Immigrants and Politics,* p. 74. This item appeared in the local paper. "We have on hand a half car of Rich nut coal which we will sell at $4.50 to close out. Edwards and Bradford M. E. Lensen, Mgr. (German)," *Tilden Citizen,* 10 March 1900, p. 5.

[11]A province of the Netherlands on the North Sea.

[12]The cheese Louise made was round, ten inches in diameter and three and a half inches thick. Interview, Ernest Ritter, February 1979.

Ritter farm in Tilden, 1902. Fritz with horses; Louise, Ernest (on her lap), Fred, Willie, Hans, Rudolf.

There are no letters for the year 1901. Her pregnancy at age thirty-eight, her ill health, and Willie's severe illness could have kept her from writing. There is still the question of whether or not it is possible for her to be happy condemned to live far from where she was born. The photograph of the family was taken in the spring of this year, so her Swiss family were able to see their home and the two boys born in Nebraska. As she told of the current happenings, Louise continued to cling to those back in the homeland. She stated: "I am very lonesome."

Tilden, January, 1902

My Dear Ones,

I begin my letter with my best wishes for the new year. May you all enter it in good health and travel through it likewise. Also, the best for your business. I still hope to hear from you on how the last year treated you. Emma wrote me that you had a baby. Best wishes to the baby girl.[1] Little Anna probably is already a good nurse maid. Now you have quite a number of boys and girls, so your business has to be good. Dear Anna, I suppose you already know that we also had a baby last summer. A dear little fellow is our little Ernest, so gay and round, just as one would wish him to be. It was a difficult birth, and I thought that I would never get back my strength. Four weeks later I had trouble with my leg, and I could hardly stand. My doctor prescribed a rubber stocking, and in a short time I was all right again. Ernest was born July 16 at 6:30 a.m. The doctor was here for eight hours, and we had to pay $15 (45 marks or 75 francs). At the end of September, our Willie got sick so quickly and badly that we were afraid we would lose him. He had to be in bed for ten weeks and was not allowed to eat solid food for twelve weeks, up until Christmas.[2]

Fritz took the children to Tilden on Christmas Eve. There was a Christmas tree in the Lutheran church. The new year came quietly to us. From Christmas until now, we have had beautiful mild weather. But today, on January 24 winter has started again. The chickens have already started laying eggs. I have sixteen to eighteen every day. They sell for 20¢ a dozen, a good price for here. I have about 100 chickens. As soon as the eggs are cheaper, we eat many of the chickens. Last summer eggs were only 5¢ for a long time. Then I did not sell any. The eggs did not keep. The heat was so great that the yolks and egg whites ran together. One hardly needed hens to hatch them! During the hottest time I had to lie in bed, and I perspired all the time. Those who had to be in the field nearly fainted. It is surprising that no one got sick. The hot winds ruined half our corn crop. My garden vegetables and the potatoes were bad. When they were in the best growth, the bad south wind singed the tops.

Maybe in the spring we will have our house and cattle photographed. You will have to have a picture of your family made also. Better still, you all come here to stay. I am often very lonesome. We are doing well here, but those who are happy in Switzerland should remain there. I don't hear a word from Brother Fritz. He must have forgotten how to write. When you have pictures of your little ones, do send me a photo. I have only Fritz and Ernst. I have pictures of all three little girls of Emma's.

Best greetings to all from your Ritter family.

Louise Ritter.

[1]Anna now had seven children. Little Anna was four years old.
[2]When he was six years old, Willie almost died from a ruptured appendix.

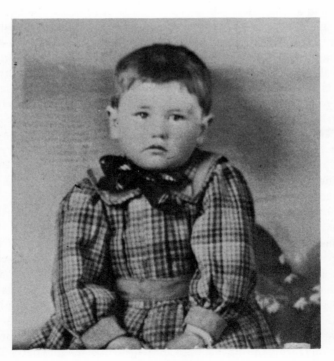

Ernest

INTRODUCTORY NOTE
For Letters of June 1 and June 20, 1902

Louise was not granted the opportunity to relax and enjoy the prosperity of the family in Nebraska. The news of the death of her younger sister, Emma, tried Louise's faith and emotional strength. Based on recent studies of death, our analysis of her responses to her grief could label them typical or atypical. However, she did not have the benefit of these studies nor the analytical approach. The death was a personal loss. Never again in this world would she see her beloved sister. Louise did have her religious faith which helped her this time and would be tested again in less than a year.

The Swiss family has tended to include among close relatives siblings and aunts and uncles.[1] Louise had had news of Emma's illness, but she had not been prepared for the death of her sister. If she had, the shock might have been alleviated; and some of the grief and recovery could have occurred before receiving news of the actual death. As it was, she felt guilt because she had not been there when her sister died. Her question is one asked often by those not present at the time of death – "Did she say my name or speak of me when she died or before she died?"[2]

Louise's religious faith helped her to accept the death. She believed that the "faithful, after bodily death, do go directly unto Christ" as stated in the Second Helvetic Confession.[3] In the future she would be reunited with her beloved sister. But she wanted to be able to assume her family responsibilities in helping to comfort her parents and care for the children of her sister.

Tilden, June 1, 1902

Beloved Parents, Brother-in-Law and Children,

Oh, Dear God, Children, now I have to write to you. Like a thunderbolt the news hit me of the death of my poor Sister Emma. I ask myself again and again – can it be possible? Or am I haunted by a bad dream? Who had known that? Oh God, how heavy rests your hand on us! I myself have felt miserable since the end of March; you'll see it in my trembling letters. I went to the doctor on Wednesday before Ascension Day, also on Sunday, May 11. Oh God, that was the death day of poor, dear Emma. If I had known that! But no little word had come to me of her long suffering. Only one week after her death, I heard from Lisabeth's relatives of her serious illness. I clung to the hope that all would be well again for her. Oh, how wrong I was! It was nine days after her death, when they at last thought to send me the news. It lies like a curse on me that they didn't notify me sooner. Brother Fritz had written a few words and our address on a mourning card.[4]

65

I hope and pray that the much too early deceased one rests in the Lord and now – while we mourn so much for her – joyously yearns for us in the eternal kingdom. May her spirit hover with blessings over her poor, bereaved husband, the poor children[5] who already in their tender age have lost their dear Mother. Oh, that poor, little boy and the dear girls – I must cry for them all day.

Dear Mother, kiss all the dear, little ones from their grieving aunt in America. And I ask you, dear Parents, to look after the poor little children as well as you can, and the Lord's blessings will rest upon you. If only we were not so far away, then I could be of some help, too. I was not able to put a flower on the dear deceased's grave. I ask you, dear Parents, to ask Sister Anna to get a beautiful wreath or bouquet for Emma's grave, and I will soon send the money.

The Lord over life and death comfort you, dear Parents, and you, poor Brother-in-law. Remember, we all have to die, and it really is a great comfort that we will all see each other again in a better world.

We all here send you greetings from the bottom of our hearts.
Louise Ritter.

Tilden, June 20, 1902

Beloved Parents,

I wrote to you on June 1 and am yearning for an answer. Did you and my poor brother-in-law find a little comfort for the sad, incomprehensible happening? To me it still seems like a bad, unhappy dream, unthinkable that my dear sister Emma is no longer with you, and that now the good Lord will waken her to a better life in eternity. In a little while we old ones will be united there where there is no separation anymore. This is sweet comfort to which we all cling.

The news of the death has shaken me no end. How it hurts to know a beloved sister is in the grave whom I had hoped so much to see one day and who hoped it, too, and wrote about it in every letter. It would have been so beautiful, but it wasn't meant to happen.

Dearest Parents, I have a question which I hope you won't forget to answer. On New Year's Eve I wrote to you and a week later to my sisters. I know that you and Anna received my letters, but I don't know if dear Emma got her letter. Ask my brother-in-law, please. How sad I would be if the beloved one had not heard from me and thought I had forgotten her. I did think of her and hers so often. Her girls are such lovely children, and the little boy resembles his mother so much, and the dear mother had to leave them all, and their father and her parents – not to see them ever again in this life. Oh, how sad I am! Who will look after them now? Oh, may God lead good people to them who will take care of them as their dear mother did. How I would love to take the sweet baby to me and be his mother. If my brother-in-law will give me the little girl, we would love to have her as our little daughter. I couldn't have a dearer reminder of my sister. If I can go once again to my dear old homeland and visit my family and put a wreath on beloved Emma's grave, Bertha could come with me. May our dear father and grandfather still live many, many years and Mother, too, so that the poor motherless orphans have their grandparents in addition to their father. Where are the four children now? Or has my brother-in-law a housekeeper? He surely cannot be without a woman's assistance. Is my sister-in-law Elisabeth with him? I heard that he has asked her. Many greetings to her. How dear Emma had to suffer last April and May. I was so sorry for her. And she had much to do with the children. Four little ones make a lot of work. Now she is released from trouble, pain, fear, and work; she is enjoying the pleasures of heaven. And we all think of her in quiet sadness after the first wild grief is gone. Was Emma always conscious? Did she think of me sometimes? Did she know she had to die? The departure from her beloved ones must have been heart-breaking. She loved them all so much, from her husband to her little ones. In God's name we have to accept it, however hard it may be. There is a reunion above the blue sky. What a comfort!

I hope you dear parents and brother-in-law and the children are all well. Everybody here is well except myself. The strength comes back very slowly.[6] You'll see by my handwriting how I tremble. Ernest is getting some teeth and is often irritable. Otherwise, he is a dear little boy and would like to walk. He pulls himself up on everything; he is very strong. Willie is also a dear one, and the other three are always in the fields. They work there with eight horses. God's blessings to you all. Do answer soon. I do hope Emma got my letter.

With dearest greetings from us to you all.

Your Louise Ritter

---

[1]Weinberg, *Peasant Wisdom*, pp. 78-79.

[2]Elisabeth Kübler-Ross, M.D., *Questions and Answers on Death and Dying* (New York: Macmillan, 1974), p. 95.

[3]John H. Leith, *Creeds of the Churches* (Garden City, New York: Anchor, 1963), p. 184.

[4]A letter announcing death comes with a black border.

[5]Emma's children – Anna, five years old; Emma, four; Bertha, three; and Fritz, a baby.

[6]Ernest had been born less than a year ago. It had been a hard birth, and her recovery was slow.

Louise's Sister Emma

INTRODUCTORY NOTE
For Letters of September 8, December 27, 1903 and January 24, 1904

The death of a child touches the deepest sources of human suffering. Louise experienced this suffering in less than a year after the death of Emma. Her ten year old son, Rudolf, was killed April 27, 1903.[1] He was driving a wagon pulled by a team of horses. A bit of hay blew off the wagon in front of the horses and frightened them. They bolted and Rudolf was thrown off the wagon and run over. A neighbor picked him up and brought his body to the house.[2] Her letters express her anger, anguish, and attempts to reconcil these emotions with her faith. She had to reach her resolution without the help of the extended family she would have had in Switzerland.

The death of a child often results in anger among the survivors; there is a wish to blame someone for the death. Recently, Elisabeth Kübler-Ross[3] and others have done much to explain attitudes towards death and to encourage us to understand our attitudes. These explanations also help us to understand Louise and her grief. Kübler-Ross explains the anger as a part of being enraged or in despair, and states one should be allowed to express these feelings. There is also the need to talk to someone about the deceased's life. The void of emptiness is felt after the funeral. The talking about the deceased reaffirms his existence.[4] Louise expressed her feelings and made continuing references in her letters to the age of this son if he had lived. Dr. George L. Engle in an article on grief indicates steps followed by an individual in resolving grief. Through her letters, it is possible to trace Louise's progression through some of these stages. First, she told of the shock, disbelief, and numbness. Then she recounted the developing awareness, the painful emptiness. Dr. Engle states that during this stage the environment sometimes seems frustrating and empty since it no longer includes the loved one. This is the period of greatest grief. The third state is referred to as restitution, the time of mourning. The rituals of the funeral serve the important function of emphasizing the reality of the death. As Louise experienced this stage, she expressed her religious belief which provided a basis for a later reunion. The next phase shifts from the personal loss to the person who is dead. Months after this there may be idealization of the dead. Louise often referred to Rudolf as the best of her children. Mourning takes a year or more, and the loss of a child has a more profound effect than the loss of an aged parent.[5] The support of relatives and friends can help, but resolution is even more difficult for Louise because her close relationships were in Switzerland.

Louise was to deal with loss through death many more times during her life, but the pain would never again be as great as it was in this situation. In working out her grief, she seemed to reach a level of acceptance. Her acceptance seemed to place death in perspective as a part of life. She acknowledged her own finiteness. Kübler-Ross states that it is important to realize whether we understand fully why we are here or what will happen when we die, it is our purpose as human beings to grow – to look within ourselves to find and build upon that source of peace and understanding and strength which is our inner selves, and to reach out to others with love, acceptance, patient guidance, and hope for what we all may become together.[6]

Louise found that inner peace and understanding and acceptance which allowed her to keep her sanity and continue to live for her husband and other sons.

Rudolf's funeral was the first in the newly organized Evangelical Friedens Church, sometimes referred to as the German church. The family had joined the church shortly after it was organized in 1902. The language and its closeness to the Reformed and Lutheran confessions had attracted them and other Swiss and Germans to the new church.

The Evangelical Catechism was based on the Luther and Heidelberg Catechism from which she would have received her instruction. Some questions and answers from the Evangelical Catechism can serve to illustrate what would have been at least a partial basis for her faith. "What must we do to be saved? We must believe on the Lord Jesus Christ."[7] "What is faith? Faith is complete trust in God and willing acceptance of his grace in Jesus Christ."[8] Especially important for her after the deaths of her sister and son would have been the questions, answers, and quoted scripture which dealt with the resurrection.

What do we understand by the resurrection of the body? On the last day Christ will raise up all the dead, as it is written in John 5: 28-29: For the hour cometh in which all that are in the tombs shall hear His voice and shall come forth; they that have done good, unto the resurrection of life; and they that have done evil, unto the resurrection of judgment.

What do we mean by the life everlasting? By the life everlasting we mean that in the resurrection all children of God shall receive the glory of Christ in body and soul and shall abide with him forever.[9]

Meanwhile, she could be comforted that Rudolf's soul was with Christ. She began to regard herself as one of the old ones looking forward to the day when all would be reunited.

Louise never allowed herself or her family to forget her "deceased darling." A large picture of Rudolf with one beside it containing an arrangement of dried flowers from the funeral were a part of the household from that time on to her death twenty-two years later.[10] Fritz died twenty-four years after Louise, and wherever he was living during those years he kept her picture and Rudolf's hanging in a conspicuous spot. The family members continued to work with horses, but each of the sons had a fear of them, and none of the children in the next generation were encouraged to ride horseback. All were warned to be extremely careful around horses. This was true even of Ernest, who was not yet two years old at the time of Rudolf's death.

These letters reveal the cumulative effect of two deaths and Louise's concern that she might also lose Fritz. What could she do if she were left alone with the four sons? She had seen death strike too often and unfairly, taking the young and the strong, not to be concerned about Fritz's health.

Tilden, Sept. 8, 1903

Much Beloved Parents,

I should have answered your dear and well-meant comforting letters long ago, but you have to forgive me when I say that the fate that has happened to me so suddenly is too hard. I believe I shall never overcome it.

Already five months have passed – I don't know how it can be possible, how I still can be alive; and yet I have to thank the Lord that He lets the time go by and with that my last hour is coming closer when I will be able to find again my darling who was so cruelly torn away from me, and that then no misfortune can separate us any longer.

I have to ask all of you dear ones not to be angry with me that I have not written. Even now I can hardly put a short letter together; it is turning and twisting in my head – oh, I have often been afraid of losing my senses. Oh, God not that also – do take me away from this unhappy world before that. How good my little boy, my Rudolf, was to me. When Ernest was crying, he often said, "Mummy, I'll do the dishes; go to Ernest." How he looked at me with his dear eyes, and now I shall no longer see those dear little stars, no longer hear his dear, happy voice! What is there still for me to do on this earth? When I gave him something or did something for him, he would thank me so dearly – no one else has ever done that. He was my best child, the merriest of the merry ones – and he was the prettiest one. And how he loved his little brother! And also Ernest was so devoted to him. And then death breaks this darling flower so mercilessly out of the circle of seven happy people –forever. My most beautiful little flower was hurt and taken into the heavenly garden we all are waiting for. Ever since, I have been thinking perhaps he had a foreboding of his early death. He often sang his Christmas verse with his gay voice: "Uh, uh, uh, I know what I do, love the Christ Child, praise the Christ Child, with all the little angels above – uh, uh, uh, I know what I do!"

Oh, yes, you darling, now you can see your dear Christ Child in the beautiful heaven above and remain there forever.

I ask you, dear Parents, to greet my brothers and sisters and to thank them

71

for their heartfelt sympathy, also Aunt Julie. I was so glad that my brother also wrote to me. I thank him for the nice picture. Are you well? I do hope so.

With hearty greetings from all of us, your –
Louise Ritter

Tilden, Dec. 27, 1903[11]

Dear Sisters and Brother-in-law,

A long and anxious time has passed since I wrote you last. You will understand that I lived through many terrible hours since then. On Christmas Eve I went with the four children to the Tilden church. The two little ones loved the Christmas tree. I was frightfully shaken, thinking of my deceased darling who a year ago recited his little Christmas verse under the Christmas tree and so soon afterwards was torn from us. Oh, hard, bitter fate!

Everybody's sympathy for us in our misfortune has moved us. Many came to our house at the time of the funeral. When we approached the church, the bells rang ten times in measured intervals, signifying the ten years of our darling. The church was full. The richly covered coffin was put before the altar. The church was decorated by the women of Tilden. The Pastor spoke such moving words that no eyes remained dry. After the service, everyone looked once more at our beloved Rudolf, passing by the coffin. This is a fine custom here. At the open grave the Pastor spoke a prayer and the Eymann sisters sang the beautiful song "In the Grave is Peace." The quiet grave that holds a piece of my life was richly decorated with flowers during the summer. But three weeks after the funeral the grave was covered with snow. At the end of April we had a bad snow storm and bitter cold.[12]

On May 9, when we were shelling corn, we had a terrific thunderstorm with rain coming so hard that we had to take the horses into the barns. In the large barn we had eight other horses, in the smaller one six of ours. In the midst of the pouring rain, lightning struck his barn and killed three horses. The hay caught fire, but fortunately the boys were able to extinguish it quickly while Father and the men took care of the horses. The horses that were killed were not ours.[13] In July, one of our horses was killed by lightning, a short time earlier, a calf in another pasture.

Now winter is reigning. New Year's Eve was like a beautiful spring day, but yesterday and today it has been bitterly cold. We already had snow in November with many cold days; the last half of December was mild.

I wonder what it is like where you are. I wish I could see your children face to face. I have pictures of only three of your children – Ernst, Fritz, and Alfred. I would be happy to have pictures of the other ones. Also, Brother Fritz has promised me a picture of his little girl. From Mother I heard what you, dear Sister, had to go through last summer. Thank God, all is well again

– I thought of you often. But I am ashamed not to have written. I hope you won't pay evil with evil, but write me a long letter soon. To all of you our best wishes for the new year, happiness and health and success in your work. May the Almighty protect you from the misfortune that happened to us last year. The year has passed, but my grief will only cease with my death. Why do you want to comfort me or perhaps blame me? Anyone who has never experienced such a misfortune, cannot comprehend it.

It is now three months since Fritz has been able to work. What will become of us if he should die? Then I would have to say often, "Happy you, Rudolf, that you were allowed to go first!"

We all stand in God's hands, and what we sow in tears will rise splendidly in great joy.[14]
Best greetings to all,
your, Louise Ritter

Tilden, January 24, 1904

Dear Parents,

It is three weeks since I wrote a letter to Sister Anna, and I hope that you also heard a bit about us. Once more I send you my best wishes; the Good Lord protect you through your whole life from all evil and give us one day a happy reunion again. Should that not happen here on earth, then in heaven in our eternal home where no far distance, no ocean, and not grim death can separate us anymore. It will not be much longer before we will be united again for man is like a flower which blooms one day and withers tomorrow.[15] We saw this again so clearly at the beginning of this new year. Our young neighbor's wife, twenty years and two and a half months old, died on January 2 giving birth to a baby girl. What a sad beginning of a new year for the poor husband, who had broken his leg seven weeks earlier. No one could remain untouched seeing the young man on crutches, limping behind the coffin. The young wife's resting place is only a few steps from our child's grave. May they rest in peace! She had sung at my Rudolf's grave. Her little child, fifteen days old, was baptised last Sunday.[16]

Yesterday I received a letter from Sister Anna which informed me that so far you all have been well through the winter. I am so glad about that. However, we here had a bad and fearful time. One night last October, Fritz stepped barefoot on two rusty nails. He had to go to the doctor because his foot and leg were very bad. So many rumors went around that neighbors and relatives asked if it were true that Fritz had to have his foot amputated. In the end, our doctor wrote an article in the paper to say how it was with Fritz.[17] That was in the beginning of November. His foot has healed now, but he still

73

has trouble walking. Everything seems wrong with his muscles. He feels weak and jittery and has no appetite. But he is getting a little better now. Of course, he could not work for many weeks, but now he does some light work, but he perspires and tires quickly. You can imagine that there is a lot of work to do. We have 185 head of cattle, small and large.

Fred and Hans are still going to school for a while. Willie goes all winter long if the weather is not too bad or if he is not sick. He is often ill. But Ernest looks well and chatters a lot. In July he will be three years old.

The first days of the new year were very cold, but then until the twentieth of the month we had real spring weather. Now it is again cold and snowing. Things are not going well with Fritz's sister Mrs. Marianne Whitwer since last fall. In October they auctioned their farm equipment since Uli had been sick since August. He will soon be sixty-eight years old. The farm will be rented to the husband of their daughter next spring. Uli is very bad.[18] He is no longer in bed; on the contrary, he does not take off his clothes any more, not even his coat. He is sick in the mind and wants to run away in the evening so that they have to use force to get him into the house. It is so sad for all.

How are your dear little ones? All busy with cheesemaking? They will visit their grandparents often. Do one day send me a picture of fat little Fritz.[19] Greetings to all. One day when the aunt from America comes for a visit, she will bring them some presents. Best greetings to our dear parents and grandparents from all of us, especially from your

L. Ritter

Greetings to Elisabeth and Fritz.

[1]The available copies of the *Tilden Citizen* for 1903 skip from March 21 to July 25, 1903. There was no reference to the death of Rudolf Ritter in the *Oakdale Sentinel, Neligh Leader* or *Norfolk Daily News.*

[2]*Interview, Ernest Ritter, December 1978.*

[3]*Elisabeth Kübler-Ross was born in Switzerland and lived there through World War II.*

[4]*Elisabeth Kübler-Ross, M.D., On Death and Dying* (New York: Macmillan, 1969), pp. 177-180.

[5]George L. Engle, M.D., "Grief and Grieving," *American Journal of Nursing,* 64 (September 1964), pp. 94-97.

[6]Elisabeth Kübler-Ross, M.D., *Death the Final Stage of Growth* (Englewood Cliffs, N.J.: Prentice-Hall, Inc., 1975), pp. 166-167.

[7]*Evangelical Catechism* (St. Louis: Eden Publishing House, 1919), p. 6.

[8]Ibid., p. 11.

[9]Ibid., pp. 56-57.

[10]Interview, Ernest Ritter, February 1979.

[11]The letter is continued in January, 1904.

[12]The *Oakdale Sentinel* and *Norfolk Daily News* report a blizzard starting April 28, 1904 with three inches of snow falling. Some was still left on May 2.

[13]Usually, farmers help each other when corn is shelled. The horses killed must have belonged to one of these helpers.

[14]The central precept from the Heidelberg Catechism and several Helvetic Confessions was God's awful and absolute sovereignty. Sydney E. Ahlstrom, *A Religious History of the American People* (New Haven: Yale University Press, 1972), p. 77.

The church was the one important institution in her life. She did not attend the Women's Guild regularly, but the October 1, 1903, minutes indicate her first participation in the organization. She made a contribution to the purchase of a Communion Service for the church.

[15]Job 14:2.

[16]The wife was one of the Eymann sisters who sang at Rudolf's grave. She had immigrated from Switzerland, and her husband was the son of Swiss immigrants.

[17]It is unfortunate that these editions of the *Tilden Citizen* are not available in microfilm nor at the newspaper office.

[18]Uli and his family had been among their first friends when they arrived in Nebraska. His wife, Marianne, was Fritz's sister. His trouble adds to the series of tragic events.

[19]Fritz is Emma's youngest child. He would be about two years old at this time.

Rudolf

75

INTRODUCTORY NOTE
For Letters of September 18, 1904, and January 8, 1905

The letters continued to be an important part of Louise's life – both writing and receiving them. But after the deaths of her sister and son, she must have realized things could never be the same. They had been away from Switzerland for over ten years. She and Fritz could never belong again in Switzerland. They had to accept that their home now was a country in which they had not been born but where two of their sons had been born. The hardships of crossing and settlement had changed them, and they had begun to establish a place in Nebraska. More and more her letters reflected her awareness that they were strangers in both lands. She did not share in the activities in Switzerland, and it was difficult to share with them the activities in Nebraska. The writing contained pleas for them to come to Nebraska, reminiscences to keep alive memories, and commemoration of anniversaries. Photographs were available at low cost, and they become an important means of sharing for the families. Also, she wrote of her continuing grief, their prosperity, the weather; and she acknowledged that she was growing old. Uli Whitwer's death helped to confirm that fact.

At the end of the September 18, 1904, letter, Louise quoted a hymn stanza which became her theme in later letters. The stanza she alluded to is the second one in the hymn which follows:

Funeral Hymn 605

Melody: Now Come, the Heathens' Savior

All believers' meeting place is there,
Where their hearts and treasures,
Where their Savior Jesus Christ
And their lives are already.

One goes here, the other there
Always to his eternal home,
Not questioned if the one or other
Were not still useful here.

Had He asked us about that,
Oh, what would we have said?
Hot with tears we would plead:
"Leave the precious soul here!"

Yet the Lord cannot do wrong;
And when it has happened,
We have nothing else to do
But to be silent and rest.

Many a heart which is no more,
We miss so deeply,
But, oh Love, we are yours,
And you want to be all to us.[1]

77

Much Beloved Parents,

Three months have already passed since I received your letter, and only today do I begin to answer it. What will you think of me! Above all, I hope that you both are well, and that you, dear Father, have fully recovered from your illness.

Our health left much to be desired. Fritz often says that he no longer has the strength and health he had before his sick leg and muscle illness brought him down. But fortunately he is much better than he was in the spring and early summer. He works all day, but he cannot do hard work any more. Also, I am not very well this year. I got ill the middle of February and lost twenty pounds in six weeks. I always felt weak and dizzy, but I have improved with time although I still don't feel well. You understand what is the matter; I feel the change of life. Our children are well and grow like the willows, like the olive tree. Hans and Fred are taller than I. Willie, who is now eight and a half years old, is also tall; and Ernest is a dear, fat little fellow. He was three in July, not four as Anna writes. And my dear, late Rudolf was only a head shorter than I. Oh, the grief, the yearning for him gnaws on me. How could a mother forget such a child as Rudolf!

Brother-in-law Uli died this summer, June 3. He had been ill for ten months. Now his wife and youngest daughter are alone in the house; the land was leased this summer. Did you hear anything about whether Elisabeth may be coming here?

We have been having beautiful weather; no rain for a long time. Because of this, the corn has grown well and is ripening. But frost may come and all must be ripe by then. Last year we had the first frost on Sept. 16, and it did much harm because the corn was still soft. In the beginning of August we threshed some oats, thirty bushels per acre on one piece of land, forty on the larger one. Wheat was a complete failure, so we had only five bushels per acre. It had started all right until black rust attacked the field before the wheat matured. The kernels dried up and nobody wanted to buy it. Newspapers warn not to feed the rusty straw[2] because cattle have died from it. Now we have to buy the flour for bread-making.[3] Let us hope for a better year next year.

Last week Fritz was in Omaha at the market with six cows and forty-four hogs. The price for hogs at present is high but low for cattle which are not corn fed. This summer he sold two car-loads[4] of cattle in Omaha which received high prices. But when the strike began, the trade was greatly damaged.[5] At present we have one hundred two head of cattle, and soon we will begin to fatten about forty with corn.

I believe if we would now come to Switzerland we would find it strange; I mean the difference in the way of agriculture.[6] How was business with my two brothers-in-law last summer as to cheese and butter? I always think they ought to be here and you, too, my parents. We hear so little from each other and that is sad. The dear children will be well and happy. Oh, if our dear Emma were still alive! But as a song says, "One goes here, the other there to the eternal home, unasked whether he is not still useful to us anymore."[7]

Greetings to all and a kiss to each child from their American aunt.

Now beloved Parents and Grandparents, write a long letter soon and be greeted and kissed from us all.

Louise Ritter

Tilden, January 8, 1905

Much Beloved Parents,

Already one week of the new year is gone. We received your dear letter on Christmas Day and two days later the fine picture of Fritz. Many thanks for it and your good wishes. We wish you, dear Parents, happiness, health, and God's blessing from all our hearts. May the future days bring you recovery from your illness, and may you still have many happy years together. I hope you will find some help until you are well again. It is hard to find someone here even for a few days. I also was not very well during the holidays, but I have to be grateful that it is not worse. I had a toothache since August. It came more frequently and harder, but I thought it might get better; yet it got worse. At Christmas (in the morning we went to church, in the afternoon was the children's service with a beautiful Christmas tree) it was very stormy and cold. For two days everything was covered with ice, and it sparkled all over. Then my pain got worse. My jaw was inflamed. So last Friday I had all my upper teeth and two lower ones pulled without suffering any pain. The dentist operated with gas; one is unconscious and in five minutes all is done. Now I have a swollen face, but hope that all will be well in a few days. Now I have bored you much too long with this, and I will quickly go to something else.

We finished harvesting the corn crop three weeks before Christmas. We harvested 6000 bushels, 30¢ a bushel. Add to that 800 bushels from fields we have leased. It will be close to 7000 bushels. With it we feed 42 head of cattle, about 70 pigs and some horses. The rest we keep for next year. A dry summer is forecast which is likely because we here in the west usually get the same weather as they had in the east in the previous year. May it come as it will; we will trust in the Lord. He will keep us in the new year; and if He should call us to Him, where could we better be than there in that home where we will be all united again, and where no death can separate us again?

I'll write soon to my sister. Best greetings to all who ask about us. Greetings to brother-in-law Fritz and his children. Please give to each of his children one of the enclosed pictures of Fred, Willie, and Ernest. The others are for you. Ernest has been wearing long pants since spring. Soon we will have a picture of him and Hans.

We had in our house a pretty Christmas tree made of cedar branches; there are no pine trees here and few are brought here.

We hope for letters from you soon, also from our grandparents.

Thousand greetings –

Your Fritz and Louise R.

and all the children.

Thanks again for Fritz's photo. I now have pictures of all four of Emma's children together and wish I could see them face to face.

[1]*Songbook* for the Evangelical Church for German Evangelical Synod of North America, trans. Maria Rosenblatt. (St. Louis: Eden Publishing House, 1908), p. 538.

[2]Both the fungus growth which grew on straw if there was moisture after it was shocked and before it was threshed and the black rust which killed the grain were dangerous to cattle and horses. Either would cause toxic poisoning and could kill the animal. Interview, Dr. Jack Cady of Arlington, Nebraska, February 1979.

[3]They took their wheat to the mill in Tilden to have it ground into their flour.

[4]A carload of cattle would be about forty-five head.

[5]The members of the Amalgamated Association of Meat Cutters and Butcher Workers of North America went on strike July 13, 1904. Vote for settlement was taken early in September when "the vote in South Omaha was overwhelming for a return to work that the leaders had little to say . . . . Dozens of union men publicly made the statement on the streets Tuesday afternoon and evening that they were going back to work just as soon as they could secure employment." "Vote to Go to Work." *Omaha Daily Bee,* 7 September 1904, p. 1.

The strike must have had an effect on the cattle market. The total cattle shipped for the week ending September 10 was 16,328 compared to 23,353 the same week a year ago. The price quoted for cattle was $5.25 to $5.85 for choice cornfed steers down to $4.25 to $4.90 for common to fair. "Omaha Live Stock Market," *Omaha Daily Bee,* 12 September 1904, p. 7. After the strike was over, the market improved. "Monday is expected to be a busy day at the stock yards and packing house. From reports received last night there will be big run of live stock today." *Omaha Daily Bee,* 13 September 1904, p. 5.

[6]The mountainous character of most of Switzerland, the high average altitude, the over-abundance of rain, and the system of small holdings prevent Switzerland from being an agricultural country. The average farm was not more than twelve acres and many were smaller than three acres. Pasture for cattle and production of cheese were most important. Potatoes, wheat, stone fruits, and vineyards were the main crops. Most of the work was done by hand because of the small farms. Martin, *Switzerland,* p. 290. In Nebraska, the Ritters continued to add to their holdings, and they were eagerly buying machinery for operating their farms.

[7]She changed the text of the stanza slightly to fit the context of her letter.

INTRODUCTORY NOTE
For Letters of March 5 and 26, 1905

The April 15, 1905, edition of the *Tilden Citizen* published a telephone directory. F. Ritter was listed as being on the same line as E. Bossard, B. Whitwer, and A. Uhlman, all friends in the Tilden vicinity. This should have made life easier for Louise and some of the other farm wives; at least they could talk to each other more easily. She did not mention the telephone, because it did not enable her to communicate with her loved ones in Switzerland.

The news of the death of her father emphasized the distance between her and the family. Her grief over the death of her father was real, but not as intense as that she expressed when Rudolf died. She had already learned to accept what she considered God's will, and there was no denial of death possible for her. She had been somewhat prepared for this death. They had been physically separated for almost twelve years, and her father had been ill often during those years. She followed a more ritualized form of grief. Much of her concern was for the one who was left – her mother. Louise knew what it was like to experience loss and the painful void after the rituals of the funeral.

Her concern for her mother reminds one of Beret in *Giants in the Earth* who grieved: "Oh, those kind-hearted parents on whom she had turned her back in order that she might cleave to him: How they must have suffered!"[1] Another character who grieved for her mother was Meta Grimsen whose "heart cried out for home. In Denmark she had left her mother, her only living relative."[2] Louise knew there were relatives near her mother who would care for her, but she still wished she could fulfill her duty as the eldest daughter and help her mother.

In the March 26 letter, Louise again wrote of the cycle of seasons which played an important role in her life. She could describe the cold and hardness of the land as Cather recorded it at the beginning of *Oh Pioneers!*: "A mist of fine snowflakes was curling and eddying about the cluster of low drab buildings huddled on the gray prairie, under the gray sky."[3] But Louise also responded to the beauty and productivity of the land as Cather's Alexandra did: "The wheat-cutting sometimes goes on all night as well as all day, and in good seasons there are scarcely men and horses enough to do the harvesting. The grain is so heavy that it bends toward the blade and cuts like velvet."[4] Louise did not write for an audience beyond those in her family in Switzerland, but her letters expressed the dramas experienced by thousands of immigrants.

All My Dear Ones and especially My Beloved Mother,

Again we have to say in our family: "It is God's will that we be parted from the dearest that we have." Oh, the message of our dear, good Father's death has deeply grieved me. Yesterday, on Saturday, March 4, I received your letter. I had such a heavy feeling in my heart, and I opened the letter with trembling and found my presentiment confirmed. Now the dear, beloved guardian of our youth has been slumbering already many a day and many a night in his last, quiet resting place. Dear Lord, receive our beloved one in your mercy, in Jesus Christ's name, Amen. God's gentle, sweet peace hover over your resting place; farewell, beloved Father. I will see you again in a better world. "The one goes here, the other there, into the eternal home, not asked if he could still be of use here." And you, dear, forsaken Mother, how sad you will be, but God won't forsake you. Through the dark valley of death He will guide those who trust in Him to His unspeakable joys and splendor.

Dear Mother, are you now going to stay alone in your present home? Oh, if we were closer, I would love to have you with us. But dear Emma's children would miss their dear Grandma. Oh yes, three years ago all was still happy with us and then sorrow came: the dear Sister, then dear Rudolf, and now our beloved father – one after the other had to depart. Yes, the earnestness of life has now come close to us so often and reminded us that we also have no permanent home here, and that we day by day shall assure ourselves of our future place. When I wrote you last January 8, I had not expected that death would come so soon, although I was worried about you, dear Sister. I always thought of you, dear Parents. How is your hurt foot, Mother? I do hope it is all right again. Oh, dear Mother, in all your letters I most enjoyed hearing that you were well, and now this had to happen. Never again can I look into the eyes of my dear father; maybe not into yours either. I shed hot tears for both of you. How can I go so far away from my children when they cry when I speak of it? But you, dear Mother can understand it. Please write me soon all about my dear Father. Did he think of me in his last days?

Many dear greetings from us all. The Lord protect you and all from all evil.

Yours,

Louise Ritter

Many greetings to Fritz Konig and children.

Tilden, March 26, 1905

My Dear Ones, Dear Sister, Brother-in-law and Children,

At last a letter again from America. On March 4, I received your letter, dear Anna, in which you informed me of the death of our beloved father. Oh, it is hard to lose one beloved one after the other, but one has to accept it and let them enjoy rest and peace. Who knows how soon we can follow them. I would like to hear soon if our dear mother is now alone in her house, or if she will move in with you or brother Fritz. If she wants to remain in Iffwyl, it would be nice for both if Aunt Julia would move to Mother; don't you agree? I believe it would be a help for both since both are lonely.

March 28. How was winter with you? Here we had no snow until a few days after New Year's Day, and it was not very cold. The coldest days were Christmas and a few days afterwards. But the second week after Christmas the snow came and lasted until the end of February. It was the coldest winter with the most snow we have had here. Day and night we had two fires going and still my hands were always cold. In some places the snow drifts were as high as a man. No one left home without a shovel. The first half of February was the coldest. For days Willie could not go to school. It is good that that time is over.

We were all well until March when we had the flu rather badly. But that is now over, too. Now in the spring it is so windy that it is not pleasant outside. The last of the wheat was sown today. We have not sown winter wheat since we have been here. If the weather permits, we will begin sowing oats. Our wheat field is forty acres; the oats field, eighty to ninety. The corn is planted at the end of April.

If you feel inclined to come to America one year, let us know in time. This year we leased two farms, and you could move into one. A few years ago Fritz bought land in two places with Uli Whitwer, and this winter he bought the other half of the property. Now Marianne does not want to talk to us anymore. We don't know why. He surely paid enough for it. No one else wanted to pay a dollar more. Their oldest daughter was on one of the places, and they wanted to buy Fritz's part from him. But they wanted to have it for nothing, and that did not work. We have to think about and take care of our children, too. Now they have moved away, about forty miles from here. We would have liked to have had a Swiss on that place, a Fritz Niklaus, somewhat related to our people who worked in a Kentucky coal mine.[5] Then his wife sent the sad news that he had died in a mine in December. How sad for that poor young woman with four little children.

You were right to use that special money for Bertha. Thousand greetings to you all. Write soon and do send us your children's pictures.
your;
Louise R.

I received the letter from our dear mother last Wednesday, and I will answer it soon. Comfort her in her great sorrow as much as possible. Visit her often.

The grandchildren won't forget their dear grandfather either. Oh, that I have to be so far away! Do come here for a year. Our Ernest is only five days younger than brother Fritz's Heidi.

[1]Ole E. Rölvaag, *Giants in the Earth* (New York: Harper & Row, Pub., 1927), p. 217.

[2]Sophus Keith Winther, *Take All to Nebraska* (Lincoln, Nebraska: University of Nebraska Press, 1936), p. 5.

[3]Cather, *O Pioneers!,* p. 3.

[4]Ibid., p. 76.

[5]Bernstadt, in Laurel County, Kentucky, (1881) was one of the most important Swiss Colonies. Wittke, *We Who Built America,* p. 301.

Louise's Mother and Father

84

INTRODUCTORY NOTE
For Letters of July 4, July 19, October 8, 1905, and January 21, 1906

The church played an important role in many immigrants' lives. Some immigrants used the movement west as an occasion to throw off the restraints of the Old World. Because of fear of their people straying away from the teachings of the church, many denominations sent out missionaries to direct the people. In their attempts to control the people, some of these denominations became puritanical and narrow in their teaching. The Old World restraints of family and tradition had been lost; the church provided these people with restraints to replace those left behind. In other situations, the church provided the people with close social ties. The ritual and the language were familiar and provided a means of maintaining ties with home.[1]

Louise and her family were together, so they did not need the restraints of the church to replace those lost from the Old World. They still had family and traditions. Other than the catechism instruction required for the boys, there seemed to be no need for an outside force to define their standards of behavior. The church was important to them for social reasons; there they found a familiar language and teaching.

The institution of the church was important to Louise, but her faith influenced her life far beyond the church boundaries. During the first decade of this century suffering was an accepted part of life, and people's belief in God and a hereafter helped them through their suffering and pain.[2] Louise's faith enabled her to regain emotional stability after the deaths of her sister, son, and father. She believed in God and a hereafter. Louise came from Switzerland where Calvinism was a national way of life in all its manifestations.[3] One expression of it was that every Christian had a calling to service and work. Louise accepted their farming as their calling. She did not complain about the work or the bad years, but she frequently expressed her acceptance that these events were the will of God. Louise found her faith liberating. She trusted that God would not give her more adversity than she could manage.

Tilden, July 4, 1905

Beloved Sister and Family,

Today, when all are celebrating the Declaration of Independence, I also want to celebrate a little, but in a different way. Jakob,[4] Fred, Hans, and Willie went to town to see the celebration. Only Father, Ernest, and I remained at home. Ernest does not feel very well today. He sometimes is

85

sick; he is growing too fast. Many thanks for the pretty picture of little Anna. I hope the others will come soon. I now have four photos. I also am longing for a picture of the cheese factory where I can see you all together.

May God help you, dear Sister, to get over your hard hour so that you all can enjoy your new little baby.[5] I thought of you with great concern since I knew you were expectig the baby since your last letter. I shall be glad to hear that all went well. You can imagine that I would have preferred to have a new child instead of losing Rudolf. But it was God's will, and He knows why He sends grief to us. He did not create us to be on earth forever, but that we should think of our eternal home and endeavor to gain it. The death of our beloved ones draws us closer to heaven above. They are released from their earthly sufferings forever, and may the Almighty be merciful to them.

While I think of it – did you receive a copy of the magazine I subscribed for for you and myself?[6] It is published in Milwaukee, Wisconsin. Let me know soon if you have not received it so that I can write to them. I am a bit disappointed; I expected a better magazine after the recommendations.

How is our dear Mother? I think she is with you now. She won't feel like coming here, just as you – oh, I can understand it. I wish you all the best in your dear old homeland, and a happy growing-up of my nephews and nieces, so that you dear Parents and Grandparents, and above all our Savior in heaven can have joy in them.

My brother's letter came almost two weeks later than yours, and I will answer it in a few days. Dear Anna, how are your parents-in-law? I no longer hear from many I knew in Switzerland. But you will understand how much I want to hear from you; especially, how our mother is getting along.

We have had a lot of rain and don't know what crops to expect.[7] It is all in God's hands. Hail has fallen near us and spoiled many prospects. May we be spared. God bless you. Best greetings and wishes from us all to all.
L. Ritter

Tilden, July 19, 1905

Dear Brother and Family,

At last I am answering your letter of June 9, and I hope that you will forgive me for being so late. Today, five months have passed since our dear, good father passed away. Oh, he will not be forgotten by any of us; the memory of him is deeply engraved into our hearts. And we are wandering towards the same destination, and in a short while we will fall asleep, never to awaken again here on earth, and blessed are those who have been ready for it, and a tear of mourning and love will be wept for us as now we weep for our father. Yes, death, the bitter death leaves deep wounds; we had to experience that three years ago.

I did not answer your letter of two years ago because everything earthly seemed so miserable, so in vain. I did not know what I would write, and I could not describe to you my boundless grief and unmeasurable mourning. You can believe that my grief for my beloved Rudolf will never cease. If you had known that dear little boy, you could easily understand. But it is a great comfort to me to know that he is with our beloved Savior, although the longing for him almost kills me. But there will be a reunion again there in that beautiful land. That is the comfort and hope for those hearts who are united in a holy faith. This is the inscription on Rudolf's grave stone.[8] We have a family lot for eight graves. I go there as often as I can. Now flowers are blooming already for the third year on the hill that covers a part of my life. Rudolf had to be the first to go from our family. God alone knows who will follow next. Oh, and our good Emma had to depart so early from her dear ones. I am so sorry for the poor little ones. If only our brother-in-law would find a good wife who would be a good mother to the children! On the 11th your little daughter was four years old; our Ernest was four years old on the 16th. All best wishes for your expected child. May it be a son this time, a little prince. I am looking forward to the picture you promised.

How is it at Anna's? I hope all are well. I am so sorry that our mother is so lonely. If we were not so far away, I would take her to me. Let me now get to the hardest part, dear Brother. Oh, how I had wished that our parents could enjoy the fruit of their work in good health for years! But God had planned it differently. Now in settling the estate, Fritz and I declare we are in accord with your arrangements and trust you fully. You say that it was our father's wish to give us 400 francs.[9] His wish is my command and sacred, but I don't think that our dear father would be angry if he knew that I would share the inheritance with my brothers and sisters or even give it entirely to you.

Tilden, Oct. 8, 1905

Beloved Mother,

At last a letter from me. I meant to write much earlier, but there was always something that prevented me from it – someone came, for two Sundays I didn't feel up to it, and on week days there is too much work. Yesterday we dug out the first potatoes. Tomorrow we should finish unless heavy rain overnight makes it impossible.

Since the beginning of September, we have had no rain and beautiful, warm weather. Last week there was much wind, and today it is especially stormy and hot. In the south it is getting cloudy and rain is threatening. If it does rain, we may get cooler weather and the first frost. The frost can no longer do any harm. Everything is ripe and the corn promises a good harvest. We do not know how much the grain will yield since it has not yet been threshed. Wheat is better this year than it was last year. We have to be satisfied and thank the Creator that He has blessed the fields so richly. The potatoes and vegetables are also good. I also picked some pumpkins last Monday. I dried some beans and some apples. It is the custom here to can vegetables and fruit in glass jars. I bought a few dozen jars and fill them every fall. So I have quite a number of rows of jars of fruit in the cellar with mulberries, rhubarb, tomatoes, apples, and peaches.

Best wishes to you on your birthday. May God keep you in good health for many more years.

Greetings to Anna and family. I will answer immediately when I receive their letter.

Excuse my scribble. Write soon again. Was your work blessed? Fritz sends extra wishes and greetings to Mother, also the boys send greetings.

Thousand greetings —
Louise Ritter

Tilden, January 21, 1906

Beloved Mother,

I received your letter by the end of the old year, and I thank you for your good wishes. We also wish our dear mother and grandmother good health and blessings for this whole year and forever, all through your life. My special wish, dear Mother, is that you can accept now your fate and be comforted by the Lord and His promises. Of course, one can never forget one's beloved ones whom death took from us. I long for my dear Rudolf and can hardly stand it, but one has to take it until it pleases the Lord to take us also to Him. He knows when our hour will strike.

January 22. How were Christmas and New Year's Day, dear Mother? I hope you spent the holidays at Sister Anna's. We had a quiet time. All December was mild. Christmas Eve we went to our beautiful new church.[10] On New Year's Day we had a little snow, but so far we have had few cold days. Just yesterday and today it has been quite raw. We read in the papers that you are suffering from great cold. These reports cause me to worry about you, dear Mother, as you are now alone in those long frosty nights. I hope there is still another family in your house.[11] I think it would be better for you if you could move to Anna, don't you? I was glad to hear that the new woman is good to you; may it continue that way.[12] The children need good supervision.

Brother Fritz will be very happy with the little prince. May God bless the children.[13]

How does it go in Ins? It will be very lively with the little folks. Are they all well? Yes, it is true Anna has not a small task. May they all stay well. Please greet them for me, too; also those in Erlach and my god-child in Messen. I am going to write her soon. I could tell and ask much more about friends and relatives, but there is not room enough in this letter. When you hear from Alex Kunz, please let me know. It must be terrible there sometimes. May God bless him in the foreign land. His family will have to endure much, too. Where is his brother Ferdinand? How is it in Mulchi? Does Elizabeth visit you sometimes? Greetings to others in Iffwyl and Jegensdorf.

Our corn crop was picked by the first week of December. It was a good harvest, a blessed year. Now we can rest a little until it is time again for the fields. At present we have more than 150 head of cattle, 90 hogs, and 130 chickens.

May my letter reach you, dear Mother, in good health. God protect you from all evil. Our children are well and happy. Hans and Willie are going to school. Write soon.

Louise Ritter

---

[1] Franklin D. Scott, "The Migration of Ideas," in *Immigration and American History,* pp. 122-123.

[2] Kübler-Ross, *On Death and Dying,* p. 14.

[3] Herold, *The Swiss Without Halos,* p. 239.

[4] Jakob was Fritz's unmarried older brother who lived with the Ritter family off and on for several years.

[5] Her sister Anna's eighth child, a girl named Emma.

[6] The magazine *Deutsche Hausfrau* was first published in September, 1904, in Milwaukee. Since she subscribed on the basis of recommendations, it seems plausible she might be referring to this publication. It was published until 1955.

[7] The rainfall was unusually heavy in 1905 – 34.60, the greatest amount recorded since they arrived in Nebraska. Leach, *A History of Antelope County, Nebraska,* p. 260.

[8] Louise at least had the comfort of the stone. Meta Grimsen is described as having to bury her infant daughter "not in the part which was gardened . . . . She was buried in the rough uncultivated space where rested all the poor; where they slept the unwaking sleep under plain board markers." Winther, *Take All to Nebraska,* p. 76.

[9] This would be nearly $2000.

[10] On April 16, 1905, the members of the Friedens Evangelical Church decided to build their own church building. They had outgrown earlier quarters. For about $3,200 a new building was erected. The membership was still mainly Swiss and German immigrants, and the services were in German. *Rooted in Faith,* p. 21.

[11] The old Swiss farm houses were built to house two or three families, each with private quarters.

[12] Fritz Konig, Emma's husband, remarried. In 1907 they had a child. Emma's children were now in a family with both father and mother.

[13] Fritz had a son, Max.

INTRODUCTORY NOTE
For Letters of July 30, August 19, and December 20, 1906

The year 1906 was a significant one for the Ritter family. That year the decision was made that Nebraska would be their home, and August 25, Fritz and his family became naturalized citizens.[1] Witnesses were Lorenz Thomsen and James Osborn. She did not tell her family, but her letters reflected this decision.

In almost every letter Louise had included a request or a hope that someone from her family would come to them in Nebraska. She felt the difficulty of maintaining a closeness with her Swiss family. She often stated: "If you could only come to us ..." or "If I could only see you to talk face to face with you." She directed some of her appeals to the nieces and nephews. She could promise them financial success, but then she would continue "but you might be unhappy here." The pattern of the letters included details about the crops and the weather, reports on the family health, in addition to her wishes that they could once again talk directly to each other. "Seasons change like people" was one expression she used to indicate her concern that she did not even know most of the children growing up in the family. Her final comfort was that there would be a reunion after death, if not before.

For the native born American, migration was the normal experience. His father was a self-made man and expected his son to do the same. Mobility was fostered by his family. The ambition of many of the immigrant fathers was to see their sons on reaching manhood established with their families on farms clustered about their own. One by one, they bought adjacent farms, the former owners joining the migration farther west. "When the German comes in the Yankee goes out" was a local proverb that varied as Swedes, Bohemians, or other immigrant groups formed the invading element.[2] Once the Ritters had made their decision to stay, the pattern of establishing their sons on neighboring farms would begin.

Louise had not persuaded anyone from her family to come to Nebraska, but two of Fritz's sisters decided to come. These women were the youngest in his family, and they would join Jakob, Fritz, and Marianne who were already in Nebraska.

Tilden, July 30, 1906

Beloved Mother,

I should have answered your letter of May 15 long ago. Excuse me for not writing before. We are just in the midst of the harvest. Wheat and oats are excellent. The wheat was perhaps better just once since we have been here. There are lots of potatoes. Also, our main crop, corn, is wonderful. But if we

91

don't get rain in the next few days, the corn, unfortunately, could be lost. This would be a great loss to the farmer. But we won't lose courage but thank our Creator and trust in Him.

How are you, dear Mother? I hope you are well. I can imagine that you sometimes go to Anna for a visit. If you could only come to us sometimes! That would be an unmeasurable joy for us and you. How Ernest and Willie would show Grandmother everything. How much questioning and answering there would be! Oh, I have imagined such a reunion more than a hundred times. I think it would be so nice, but many a tear would also flow for the ones who have died. Did you, dear Mother, also hear that Rosetti and Elise intend to come here with their families? For these people it surely will be easier to advance here than there. We will always respect and love our dear, beautiful homeland, but because of the way of farming there and the annoyance with help – I don't think that any one single person of us would be inclined to change. I would much rather have had you all here in our vicinity. Healthy people, especially if they have money to invest, have no difficulty securing land here. We would be so glad to have relatives here, for we are entirely surrounded by American people.[3] Last spring the Uhlman family, good friends of ours, moved to Oregon. There have been many changes here the last year, almost all are now strangers around us. And next spring there will be more changes.

I would love to visit once again my old homeland and even more the dear people whom I still have over there, above all our dear mother and my dear brothers and sisters with their children. At the dairy the expected event will be over. If Elisabeth is there, please give her my greetings. We would enjoy it if she would write to us. If no one visits us next Sunday or a week later, I intend to write to Sister Anna. How are they all? I don't hear from Brother Fritz. It has been a long time since he promised me a photo of their home and of their family. I hope he will send us one. Is Cousin Alexander back from Russia? I can well imagine that Elise Marti loves her little son. Best wishes to her and God's blessing. Has Fritz married? I think if I would visit you now much would be changed.

Grandmother would not know little Fred and Hans now that they have become young men of eighteen and nineteen. Willie was ten in March, and Ernest five on July 16. Oh, he is a darling boy, bigger than many seven years old. Willie goes to a German[4] school in Tilden. The Pastor teaches there. He rides to school three and a half miles, or one hour and twenty minutes. Willie is also tall for his age, and all the boys are well at present. If it doesn't get worse, Fritz and I can't complain. The great heat often makes us feel miserable. But tomorrow is already August 1. When that month is over, cooler days will come, and before one realizes it, winter will have started its regime. May it be a mild one for us and you. Seasons change like people, joy and sorrow. July 15 a man, thirty-four years old from Tilden, drowned in the

Elkhorn River. He was a good swimmer, but he got a cramp. On July 24 in Tilden a ten and a half year old boy died from tetanus. He had had a splinter in his big toe. Another accident or crime happened in May in Tilden. A bachelor painter burned with his small home on a bright morning. His arms and feet were like coal – a terrible sight. An autopsy showed a gun-shot wound in his head, and now they don't know whether it was murder or suicide. These are all sad happenings. I have to close now and hope to hear soon from you, dear Mother, and get good news.

Best greetings to all brothers, sisters, and relatives – whoever asks about me. Best greetings to our dear mother and grandmother from all of us. Louise Ritter

Tilden, August 19, 1906

Dear Sister and Family,

It has been a long time since I wrote to you last. Perhaps you would be interested to hear from us. Three weeks ago I sent a letter to our dear Mother. You most likely heard about that. That week we had worked hard with harvesting. Thank God, that is done now. We want to be able to thresh soon after the harvest, so we put it up in piles. Three, four or more bundles are put up close together. This is called a shock. Then a steam engine is brought and the threshing goes fast and neatly.[5] This year we have perhaps fifteen loads of oats. There are still bundles lying around the field which will add to the stacks. In five or six weeks the oats can be threshed. The weather then is cooler and the threshing and cooking are easier than now in the terrific heat.

Last Monday, July 13, we shelled the rest of the corn and sold it immediately.[6] That also was the coolest day of the week. Afterwards a real heat wave started. It has been 100 degrees in the shade. In the kitchen it was often 112 degrees, and what it was like in the sun! The men were always so wet that their shirts were as if they had been drawn from the well. For three days they could only begin working after four in the afternoon. Fortunately yesterday an electric storm cooled the tremendous heat with rain.

Now I will describe to you the better side of our farm life, for I would be so pleased if you could decide to come here. One can make money here easily. Already for nine years we have had good harvests,[7] and this year the corn will be excellent unless hail damages it. This God may prevent. All that we have sold has paid well. The corn we sold last Monday yielded $610. In addition, we sold this summer 100 hogs and 45 head of cattle (42 bulls, 3 cows), all fed with corn we raised. We received $4000 for them. Now we have 130 to 140 head of cattle. There are 34 young calves, only one is all red; the others have all or partly white heads, white faces – it is a pretty sight. How your boys

93

would enjoy it if they could also have such a big, beautiful herd of cattle on a nice Nebraska farm.

Dear children, tell your dear parents to come also to America and to bring dear Grandmother with them! From all my heart I wish to see once more my beloved ones in my old homeland and to meet their children. Oh, do come here! Fritz's sisters Rosetti and Elise are coming here next spring, perhaps also Elisabeth. Is she now in Iffwyl? The photo you sent me last spring is a great joy to me. I look at it often. I still know you Anna and Ernst quite well; the children I have to guess. Will I receive one day a picture of the other children? I am afraid not. How are Fritz and family? Are they well? They will enjoy their little son.

While I think of it: Do you get the women's magazine I ordered for you regularly, and do you like it? Please answer me honestly. I hope Mother reads it too.

August 27. When I wanted to mail my letter last week, I did not have a single envelope so I had to wait until someone went to town. On Thursday the whole state had a big rain. Fred read this in the paper. It got much cooler; this morning the thermometer read only 8 degrees above the freezing point. We do hope it does not frost for quite some time. If we had frost now, no corn would be ripe and the stalks would make bad fodder. Our people are cutting now and will be finished with stacking hay for next winter. There is not much hay. Many cattle will have to do without hay next winter, and we will have to be satisfied if we have sufficient straw. We don't keep more cattle than we have barns and fodder for. Many Yankees and Irish people here don't care if they have even a protective wall for their animals, much less barns to keep them warm.

Do write soon and tell me how you are and what the cheese trade was like this summer. I hope the best for you, for everyone who works deserves his reward. If you have a hard time to earn money, you ought to come here. Your boys and girls would have a better future here. But do as you like. We would earn little thanks if we would entice you to come here. No one likes it here in the beginning.

We are well and hope the same for you. Many greetings to all and write soon.

Louise Ritter

Tilden, Dec. 20, 1906

Beloved Mother,

With giant steps, the old year comes to an end. I am almost afraid that my lines won't reach you this year, dear Mother, but I hope that my little letter will be forwarded to you in Ins.

Dear Mother, my best wishes for the new year. May the dear Lord bless and protect you and keep you well, and your children and grandchildren of whom we think with such love.

How happy we would be if you would come to us next month also. Then you would no longer be so lonesome. You know that on Jan. 19 Rosetti and her people will embark and Elisabeth will live in Ersigen. The departure will be hard for them. Jakob bought for them the late Uli's farm. They will live twenty minutes from us. We will pass them on our way to town. We own a farm closer to town which Jakob took on lease last spring.

On December 1, we finished harvesting our corn. The yield was good. The grain harvest was also plentiful, but the hay was poor. We will have to feed straw with the hay to our 150 head of cattle and then ten to twelve horses. We had a very good apple crop last summer. The other fruit was plentiful also. It is a joy to walk through the woods along the brook and see on all sides plums, cherries, and grapes. This splendor is long gone. Now another tree, the most beautiful one on earth, keeps all hearts in Christendom and especially the little ones in feverish excitement. In our church the Christmas service will be the last Sunday in the old year since our congregation is without a pastor at present.

December 24. Yesterday afternoon we decorated a little tree for our boys – not a pine tree but a cedar tree! It will be a joy for the little ones this evening when it shines with candle light. When you get these lines, dear Mother, the festive days of the Blessed Christmas season will be over and the new year will have come.

May the memory of past joys bring you blessings. Since you plan to go to Ins for some time, I'll send my letter there. Perhaps I'll hear from you from there, and from the other people. We would enjoy that. Up until now we have had beautiful weather with no snow. Today it looks like snow, and we will have a white Christmas after all. Willie goes to school alone this winter. There are only ten pupils. Next fall Ernest can go. He is already old enough and a big boy, and a dear one, too. Fred and Hans help Father a lot. They picked the corn all by themselves. Dear Grandma wouldn't recognize these two boys anymore. It would be the same with me with the boys I last saw in my old homeland.

There is not much news from here. Each day brings us closer to our destination. I am not too well; a certain weakness and tremble bothers me all the time. But I am glad if it gets no worse and I don't need help. Perhaps it will get better in summer – as God wants it. I'll keep still. Fritz feels well. I hope my lines find you in good health. I also wish God's blessing and happiness and health to my dear sister and her family for the new year. I'll write again when there is some news.

I want to ask you one thing. I cannot get a nice black cap here. Perhaps Rosetti could get me one from Sister Anna in Goldback and find a little place for it among her things. If Anna can make me one, Rosetti should give her an

95

extra franc for the material and her work. I would like a good cap, not too flat. If Anna has no time, she should let it go. If Rosetti could bring a pretty shawl embroidered with roses and lined with black wool, I'll pay for it. Please, ask if she can do it and has room for it; otherwise, she should forget about it.

Again my best greetings from all to all.

Fritz and Louise Ritter

[1]The Swiss ranked third in the average length of residence in the United States before becoming naturalized citizens. The Germans and Swedes ranked first and second. The Swiss ranked fifth in percent of those in the United States becoming naturalized (72.6%). The Danes, Swedes, Germans, and Norwegians had a greater percent. Bernard, Zeleny, and Miller, eds., *American Immigration Policy,* p. 145.

[2]Hansen, *The Immigrant in America,* pp. 61-62.

[3]In Swiss villages friendship ties are said to be found most often among kinsmen. The lack of relatives nearby contributed to her loneliness. Weinberg, *Peasant Wisdom,* pp. 80-81.

[4]The pastor left in November 1906 and they had no pastor until October 1907. Willie's German school was over until catechism began.

[5]"In eastern Nebraska where the binder was used, two different ways of threshing were followed. The first was threshing from the shock. As soon as the grain had cured well in the shock, the thresher began at one end of the neighborhood circuit – or with the man who was most importunate – and, after his threshing was done, moved from farm to farm until the last one was finished. In a wet July, the shocks would soak up rain until it was necessary to take off the cap sheafs and perhaps tear the shocks partially down to dry them out. With continued wet weather, the wheat would sprout in the shock, extensively damaging the value of the grain . . . . Threshing from the field, as it was called, made it possible to market the grain at once and secure often needed cash or flour to be made from the wheat. When threshing from the field, a farmer engaged about six or seven men with their teams and bundle racks. Usually three men without teams pitched bundles onto the wagons from the shock. Two men with box wagons and scoop shovels hauled the threshed grain to the granary . . . .

The second method was to thresh from the stack. In this case, as soon as the grain was cured in the shock, the farmer stacked his bundles and waited to thresh until fall, when the weather was cooler. An advantage of this scheme was that one could put his shocks into the stack and not chance having the grain damaged while waiting for several days, or even weeks, for his turn at the machine. It was not thought wise, however, to place too many stacks in a stackyard because lightning sometimes struck one stack and destroyed all of them; . . . ." Dick, *Conquering the Great American Desert,* pp. 314-315.

[6]Corn prices ranged from 36¢ to 39¢ a bushel. *Neligh Leader,* 10 August 1906, p. 1.

[7]Recorded statistics on rainfall support her comments. From 1897 and 1906 rainfall ranged from 20.81 to 34.60. Leach, *A History of Antelope County, Nebraska,* p. 260.

INTRODUCTORY NOTE
For Letters of February 24 and July 28, 1907

Fritz's sisters, Rosetti and Elise, arrived from Switzerland, and Louise understood their difficulties in adjusting to Nebraska. They brought reminders of Switzerland; of special importance was the picture of her father. Pictures of her deceased ones kept their memory alive and in a sense kept them alive for Louise. Pictures of her nieces and nephews helped her feel a part of their lives. Even more exciting for Louise was to have visitors from her side of the family. They were not from Switzerland, but cousins from Columbus, Ohio. No matter how distant the relationship, the loyalties of kinship were important to her.

Tilden, February 24, 1907

Beloved Mother,

How long you will have waited, day by day, for an answer – and in vain. Last Saturday I received that nice picture of our father. Many, many thanks to you, dear Mother, for the best present that you could have given me. How much he looks like himself on that picture; it is as if he could start to speak. A great yearning for him comes over me when I look at his dear face. We also have a large picture of our Rudolf.

I did not receive your letter until February 19. Rosetti[1] could not find the letter and was afraid it was lost. But she found it finally. I must explain to you, dear Mother, why the picture and letter did not get to me earlier. The new immigrants had a long and hard journey. It seems as if the agent had cheated them. In New York they were kept from Sunday or Monday until Thursday because something with their tickets was not in order. It was not until the evening of February 3 that they arrived in Tilden at last. All complained that they didn't feel well. The poor little child still is not all right. She coughs and cries a lot; her smile is so sweet but she looks so tired. They all say that she is not at all as she was in Switzerland. They could not get into their house until February 15. That is the reason I got the picture so late; they could not unpack any sooner.

We butchered and made sausages last week and that delayed my answer. Last Monday we sold seventeen cows in Omaha. Fritz went with them and returned last evening. Rosetti was with me on Monday. Everything is so strange to them, and they will feel that way for a long time. Elise is not well and complains of a stomach ache.

The first days of this month were rather cold, but then the weather was fine and warm, so they already spoke of planting. Now it seems that March will bring the wind and cold that February missed. I often worried about you, dear Mother, when I read about the hard winter in Europe. But Rosetti and Mr. Strahm[2] comforted me by reminding me that in Switzerland people don't die from freezing. I am relieved to hear that Fritz has a good wife and that both along with the children will look after you. I can imagine that a step-mother does not have an easy task with a group of children. It is all the better for both sides that you, dear Mother, speak with appreciation of the step-mother of Emma's children. Emma is far away from many troubles and sorrows of this earthly life. She hardly would want to change with us. Brother Fritz should not forget you, Mother; but he doesn't write to me either. But he ought to think of you always. How is Anna with her beloved ones? I will answer soon, and may these lines meet you in best health.

Please excuse me since I am so late with my answer. My thanks again for your dear present. I will honor it always. The Lord bless and protect you, dear Mother. Friendly greetings to Anna and all. I would enjoy it if one of the children would enclose a little note.

Best greetings and love,

Louise Ritter

Tilden, July 28, 1907

Beloved Mother,

I received your letter on July 3 and enjoy reading it again and again. I am so glad that you, dear Mother, are well and also to hear so many good things about my little nephews and nieces. But it hurts not to know these dear little people; I have not even seen a picture of most of them. I have photos of all of Emma's children, none of Fritz's, although he has promised them to me long ago. And I have not received one of Anna's girl, Emma. Well, what hasn't happened until now the future may bring. I do hope so.

Dear Mother, perhaps you have heard already the news from Aunt Julia. On June 22 I received a letter from Columbus, Ohio, and I thought immediately it was from Uncle Alfred.[3] He wrote of his children coming to visit. Sunday evening on July 7, they arrived here from Omaha (145 miles east of here) where they had visited a friend. I enjoyed their visit very much as you can imagine. They were the first relatives of my side who visited me in this country. They were Anna, the oldest one who is twenty-five years old; Paul, nineteen years; and Lina, sixteen years. Adele, twenty-three years old, did not come. The girls have real Kunz faces with blond hair and blue eyes. Paul, however, is dark like his mother. They brought pictures of their parents. I loved all three of them; they are dear girls and Paul is a good boy. Anna works at a railway company as a secretary and earns $66 a month. Paul works at an electric plant and also earns a high salary. Uncle was able to get free tickets for Paul and Lina, and Anna could buy her own ticket. Columbus is about

1000 miles from here. I hope that next year their father will visit us. Last Monday I received a letter and two cards from them telling me they arrived home safely.

Perhaps you heard from Elisabeth that little Anna got a sister on July 9. Lina and the child are well, but it is rather hard on the young woman to have two children in eleven months. Anna is still very little and cannot walk yet. Rosetti has a lot to do. Lina can soon work again and help her mother.

So far we have had many electric storms. When the child was born, there was a severe storm the whole night and another one in three days. The next week we were driven out of our beds three times, and the storms lasted through the day. Last Tuesday evening we again had terrible weather for about an hour.

[1]Rosetti Ritter Kunz was forty-four years old when she arrived in Nebraska. Her brother Fritz was six years older than she. See Appendix II for the list of Fritz's brothers and sisters.

[2]Gottfried Strahm was the husband of Rosetti's daughter, Lina, and the father of the child who is described as being so ill.

[3]Alfred Kunz was Louise's mother's brother who lived in Columbus, Ohio.

Fritz Ritter's brothers and sisters. Left to right, back row Fritz, Elise, Jakob; front Marianne, Elisabeth. Anna and Rosetta are not present.

INTRODUCTORY NOTE
For Two Letters of December 21, 1907

Louise's description of the sudden death of Elise's husband started a review of the sudden deaths that had occurred the past year. She used no euphemisms to cover the fact of death, nor did she indulge in a morbid preoccupation with death.

She quoted the stanza from the hymn reminding the reader that we are not asked if we still need the deceased one, but the living must behave with patience and dignity. Her comfort was in her religion. She believed in a heaven where those who had suffered on earth would be rewarded, but Rudolf's tragic death would always haunt her.

She shifted suddenly to the events of the past months. The letters were quiet and reflective in tone. The holiday season was a time for reminiscing. In Switzerland between Christmas and New Year's Day a traditional meal called raclette (melted cheese served with boiled potatoes and pickles) was often shared by family, relatives, and friends. This expressed the unity of the group to the outside world.[1] Her expression of unity was through the letters.

Fritz was acquiring more land, hopefully for his sons to farm. But he shared with Louise by buying household conveniences and luxury items. She was proud of their prosperity; she would liked to have shared it with the other dear ones.

Tilden, December 21, 1907

May the Lord give you a Merry Christmas and a Happy New Year! Beloved Mother,

Today I received a letter from Sister Anna, and if sleep doesn't overcome me, I will also answer that letter this evening so that it can be mailed tomorrow. I have been yearning for news from you. Perhaps I'll hear from you on New Year's Day. I do hope these lines, dear Mother, will reach you in good health, just as they leave us.

The old year comes to an end and the new year enters. May God, the Lord, also keep and protect you in the new year and bring to you much joy and happiness and to your children and grandchildren. The good Lord may give strength also to those who have to bear great sorrow and who have not been able to recover from their hard fate.

You will have heard how unexpectedly Elise's husband passed away.[2] On August 25 he had a stroke. I will never forget how Elise screamed when I went over to her in the afternoon: "They took my husband, my dear husband!" It was terrible, and in the beginning we feared she would lose her mind. Now she is somewhat calmer, but she almost grieves herself to death. Yes, such a grief almost breaks the human heart; the world turns dark when the grave closes over a beloved one. It would be unbearable if one could not find comfort in the Godly promises. In that beautiful land is comfort and hope for the hearts which were united in the holy faith. We feel sadder and yearn more for our late beloved ones when the year comes to an end. We consider that time a milestone in our lives which warns the thinking man.

Last summer in our neighborhood were several unexpected deaths. In the beginning of August an eighteen-year old girl drowned in a river eighteen miles from us. The other day, two or three miles away, a youth of about the same age who was the only support of his widowed mother drowned. The girl's accident was especially tragic. Two sisters and a young laborer of her father's were pushed backward over the bridge by a horse that had become frightened by the buggy. The horse struck out wildly and made it impossible to rescue the girl in the river, which was fifteen feet deep. For three and a half days they could not find the poor girl; thirty men searched for her.

But now enough of these sad events; we have to enjoy the good in life and be thankful for it. The year that soon comes to an end has given us many good things. Although the crops were only mediocre,[3] the prices were high, and the fruit excellent. With thankful and praying hearts we will begin the new year. If the Lord is with us, nothing will fail.

In three days Christmas will be here. The church service begins at 7:30; it takes half an hour to get there. It will get late; may it not be too cold. Ernest can hardly wait; Willie will recite his verses. The two little boys attend school regularly and have not missed a day since October when it began. If only it were not so far; two miles or forty minutes is too long for those little ones in bad weather. We keep them home when it snows. We had the first snow December 13, and it is still on the ground. If it doesn't get worse, we can stand it. How is it with you? Please write soon telling how you are and the little ones at the dairy. Let the girls write a little note and enclose it in Grandmother's letter to faraway America. If we could only speak together once again in our lives! There is so little one can say in a letter. One gets old and has so little of each other. And one goes here, the other there, into the eternal home without asking if he or she could still be useful here. Do Elise and Rosetti from Jagenstorf visit you sometimes? Give them my greetings, also Elisabeth Ritter. Are you staying in your present home?
Best greetings to all
Louise Ritter

Tilden, December 21, 1907

Dear Sister and Family,

Soon the old year will end, and it is time that you should hear from us again. Your children will be looking forward to Christmas with impatience as Willie and Ernest are. But when these lines reach you, the festivities will already be over, but the joy will linger on. Perhaps dear Mother and Grandmother will be with you as last year. I enjoyed the letter so much telling such nice things about your children. Continue, you dear nephews and nieces to give joy to your parents and grandmother and to be helpful, and the Christ Child and God will be happy about it, too. How will my dear Rudolf celebrate Christmas up above in the eternal light? Do you know, Anna, that Dec. 27 is his birthday, and he would be fifteen years old if he were still alive? Sister-in-law Elise Friedli will be lonely this Christmas and New Year. Although she is with other people, her thoughts will always be with her late husband. It is hard for her, and I am sorry for her. We will ask her and Rosetti's family to celebrate New Year's Day with us.

On December 24, at 7:30 we will celebrate Christmas in our church. Willie will help there for the first time. Ernest didn't want to. That sweet little fellow chatters gaily in English! For three months now he has gone to school with Willie without missing a day. Wouldn't you dear Swiss nieces and nephews like to come to America and learn to speak English? You would enjoy that. You know, Sister Anna, I would love it so much if all your children who can would write me a little letter. Do try if you can make them do that. How was your business this year? And your health? I haven't heard from Mother lately. Did the cards arrive? How are Brother Fritz and family? Perhaps I'll hear something about our relatives from you. How are the children of our late Sister Emma? How I would love to see you all again if it weren't for that terrible long trip. But perhaps you'll come here one day. God alone knows what will happen.

Now about our news. This year all the crops were mediocre, but the prices high, so we can't complain. We also hoped to yield much from our hogs. We had 120 hogs, but with the cholera we have to be satisfied to have 40 left.[4] Many neighboring farmers fared worse, having hardly ten left out of a big herd. We have all sorts of implements on our farm. Last month, Fritz bought a gasoline motor to pump water on still days, on windy days the wind pumps. For two years we have used an elevator so the grain and corn need not to be shoveled anymore. It saves a lot of hard work. No other farmer around us has such an elevator. In addition to my washing and sewing machine, I now have a dough kneader.[5] I have been using it for two months and am very satisfied with it. Fritz is thinking of buying still another farm after the new year begins. The price has gone up a lot. A somewhat good farm costs $11 to 12,000, and Fritz wants to buy a good one.[6]

We have enjoyed the last three months since there is not as much work to do as in the summer. I go with Fritz to town once in a while. I received my Christmas present – a beautiful fur for $5 (15 francs). Ten days ago we had the first snow; since then the days have been cold but there has been little wind. After it snowed Hans went rabbit hunting. He brought seven home last Friday. Hans, your godchild, is a big, fat fellow weighing 165 pounds. Fred is taller but slimmer.

And now my best wishes for the new year. God's blessing be with you always. Best greetings from all of us.

Louise Ritter

Do answer soon!

[1]Weinberg, *Peasant Wisdom,* pp. 72-73.

[2]Elise Ritter Friedli and her husband Gottfried came over with Rosetti's family on January 28, 1907. Elise and Gottfried had been married on November 23, 1901. He died August 25, 1907.

[3]Rainfall was considerably less than the year before when she wrote in glowing terms: 1906 - 29.16; 1907 - 17.96. Leach, *History of Antelope County, Nebraska,* p. 160.

[4]"The livestock industry recovered rapidly from the depression of the Nineties. The development of a serum for hog cholera, long the bane of the swine industry, greatly reduced the ravages of that disease, and the number of hogs on Nebraska farms increased ... to a high of 2,435,351 in 1907, after which there was a decline." Olson, *History of Nebraska,* p. 263. One wonders if Fritz had not yet found or used the serum.

[5]A bread kneader resembled a large flour sifter. There were prongs that turned and worked the dough. It was easier than kneading by hand, especially if a person had any rheumatism. Interview, Mrs. Olga Ritter, January 1979.

[6]Based on 1920 census Swiss immigrant farmers ranked high (upper one to seven) in total farm value in land and buildings and average value per acre. Edmund DeS. Brunner, *Immigrant Farmers and Their Children* (Garden City, New York: Doubleday, Doran and Company, Inc., 1929), p. 46.

INTRODUCTORY NOTE
For Letter of June 11, 1908

Fifteen years have passed since Louise and her family immigrated to Nebraska. In her last letter she stated: "There is so little one can say in a letter. One gets old and has so little of each other." Two deaths in Switzerland during the past year and another birth emphasized the passage of time. She had never denied that their life in Nebraska was easier than it would have been in Switzerland, but she did reflect: "Had I known fifteen years ago that you, dear ones, would not come here, or we would not return, I believe I would never have come to America. Life is good here, but one ought to see each other once in a while." The tone of the letter reflects more contentment than many of the others, but it is almost fatalistic: "Man plans – God leads often in very different ways."

Her letters during these years often include statements revealing her difficulty in keeping the closeness between the two groups. In the December letter of this same year she pleaded: "Don't be cross with me, dear Anna, that I write so little. My thoughts are with you every day." The same concern is voiced in the January 1, 1912 letter. "Oh, how I wish I could chat with you instead of sending my scribble."

Tilden, June 11, 1908

Beloved Mother,

A week ago I received your letter, and I want to answer it immediately. You can see that we are still alive in spite of the bad news in the papers. Nebraska is a large state and no week passes without bad news from one or more places of storm damages, not to speak of other states. May the Almighty continue to protect us.

I do hope that the bad pains you complained about, dear Mother, have subsided. They were most likely nerves as with Godmother Julia. I suffer from it, too, sometimes. It is as if the pain jumps from head to limbs and vice versa. I wish you quick recuperation.

I don't know if Uncle Alfred will visit us. Anna and Paul spoke of it on their Easter cards. We haven't heard anything since then. It is sad that Uncle Rudolf had to suffer so much, and I wish him heavenly peace and sweet rest. His boys have been married for some time. You wrote of the death of a Mrs. Marti Sutter. Do you mean Lisabeth Schuried? I thought her father, the teacher, had died long ago, but I may be mistaken. Sister-in-law Elisabeth will rest in peace, too. When we heard of her bad arm, we guessed that she was not well.

I passed on your greetings to Rosetti and Lina, and they send you greetings also. Rosetti says that she likes America quite well and does not wish to

105

go back. Elise says she wants to return next spring. I don't know. Man plans – God leads often in very different ways. Had I known fifteen years ago that you, dear ones, would not come here or we would not return, I believe I would never have come to America. Life is good here, but one ought to see each other once in a while. Do you know that Lina has two children? This year a third one is on the way, perhaps in the fall, maybe earlier. They complain now of too much work – how will it be when there is one more child? They come to see me very seldom. Don't mention anything in your next letter that I said something. One never knows who gets these letters to read. They are not all as Elisabeth was and Fritz is. They are the best of all the brothers and sisters in the family. By the way, Jakob is now more friendly to me and the boys.[1] Perhaps he sees in others things which do not please him. He works at our 120 acre farm. Perhaps in the spring he will move to town, buy himself a nice little house and rest. He also gets older and older.

Our Willie was twelve years old in March, and today he is working in the field for the first time with two horses. He quite likes it, and Ernest thought he could cultivate too. He is bored at home. So he often goes with the others into the field[2] or plays at home with the cats and dogs. Ernest will be seven next month. He is big and strong. Last winter he couldn't go to school for many weeks because of sick eyes. Often he could not keep his lids open because they hurt him so much. The doctor did not know what it was. He prescribed dark glasses. He is not wearing them now, and for the last two weeks his eyes have seemed to be all right. His problem started after the new year began, and it got slowly worse, and now it is gone. May it never come back again.

Fred and Hans are also working in the field, so it is the first time that Fritz can rest a little. Fritz can't walk very well; his feet hurt him so much. Willie can ride on the corn cultivator. The corn is still very small. We had the longest rainy spell since we have been here.[3] It was cool and the corn grows better in warm or hot weather when it is wet enough. The oat and wheat fields are fine and so is my garden. My house plants bloomed all winter and were a joy. Now the blooming starts outside. We had an exceptionally mild winter and little snow. But spring was cold, so one could think he was in the midst of winter. It is with us as with you; beautiful warm days that change quickly to ice and frost. On Easter Sunday it was hot like summer; the following week we had to heat the house. The fruit trees were in full bloom, but only the last blossoms were spared from frost. Along the creek there are many plum and cherry trees and grapes. The beautiful plums are all damaged, but there are many cherries.[4] They are not fit to eat, but they make excellent jelly, and they are good boiled if one does not spare the sugar! Was it so bad in Switzerland that the late frost did a lot of damage? It would be too bad, but it can't be helped. Your letter must have been written before the disaster.

I had to interrupt my writing for an hour to go to the field, and I also cleaned a dish of strawberries. Hans planted them; he is a good gardener. Every free minute he runs into the garden to hoe or plant or just to see what is growing. Fred does not care for that. He prefers to read about railroads, electricity, or such. He says he wants to work on the railroad.[5]

So Sister's family has a new member.[6] Good luck to them and the little new baby and strength and courage to Anna in her hard task to raise her children properly. Her work will never end. I wish I could see all her children. They will still be in Ins; at least you did not mention that they moved. I have often thought of Anna. I will write soon. My best greetings to them and Brother Fritz and family. They must have forgotten how to write; it is really sad to be so learned and never find time to write to us. If he does the same with you, dear Mother – that would really make me angry.

With best greetings and wishes
Your
Louise and family
Write soon!

---

[1]Jakob never married and lived with Fritz and Louise many years. Jakob was a morose man, often critical of Louise and the boys, expecting them to work all the time. Interview, Ernest Ritter, December 1978.

[2]The men took a morning break at nine and an afternoon break at four. Ernest tells of carrying a lunch to the field, including a pail of wine. He was swinging it around and spilled some of it. His older brother Hans asked why he just didn't dump it all out. He did – and ran home as fast as he could. Interview, Ernest Ritter, December 1978.

[3]It might have been the longest, but it did not result in the most rain. However, the year before had only 17.96 and 1908 had 27.95, so it could have seemed the worst.

[4]The cherries were chokecherries, which grew wild along the creek and still grow wild some places in Nebraska.

[5]Fred never worked for the railroad, but he had a lifelong hobby of reading about railroads and collecting railroad materials.

[6]Anna's last child was Klara, making her family total nine children, five boys and four girls. (Ernst, Fritz, Walter, Otto, Anna, Alfred, Martha, Emma, Klara.) It seems strange that she did not name one daughter after her sister, Louise.

INTRODUCTORY NOTE
For Letter of December 26, 1908

Louise did not make a direct statement that the old days were being challenged, but she did tell her sister that as the children left home and attended school, problems began. Louise was proud of the children's ability to speak English, but she must have realized that if their European values were to survive in America the preservation of their language was essential. Speaking Schweizerdeutsch in the home was hardly enough to counter the effects of the many contacts which the children experienced with the American born, especially in the school.[1]

As a rule American public schools took no account of the cultural background of the children but shaped the children of all nationalities according to the American mould. Rarely, if ever, did a school make any attempt to utilize the customs of the foreign born in school activities. If this had been done, the culture of the community would have been enriched, and the children would have seen importance in the culture of their foreign born parents. Instead, the school increased the strain between the foreign born parents and their American children.[2]

The widening of the interests of the children left Louise more alone. Also, there had been changes in the community. Many who shared her Swiss background and language had left. In rural and small town Nebraska, no genuine invitation was extended to immigrants and their children to become structurally assimilated.[3] A perusal of the local paper reveals that the social activities centered around the townspeople. Seldom did the name of a foreign born appear unless in an obituary. Her circle included those back in Switzerland, new neighbors, her family, and the church. Even a revival of the hope of returning to Switzerland was regarded with mixed feelings. She knew she would be an outsider there also. Rudolf was the only one who was not growing away from her; she would not let his memory fade.

Tilden, December 26, 1908

Much Beloved Mother, Sister, Brother-in-law and Children,

Friday, Dec. 18, I received a letter from our dear mother. On Dec. 22 I sent the card, and now finally comes the promised letter which I am sending to Ins as Mother suggested. I hope darling Mother will still be with you when my letter arrives.

The Lord's blessing to you for the new year. May He protect you now and always. Many thanks, dear Mother, for all your good wishes. Blessings also to Emma's dear children. Christmas has passed; may the memory of it linger for many years. If the calendar had not indicated Christmas, we could have thought it was spring. For many days it has been so mild. Altogether we have

109

had few cold days and only little snow. But we can still have a lot of winter weather because it is a long time to spring. I hope that you don't have too cold a winter now after New Year's Day since you have already had severe winter days.

Dear Anna, every day you are sending a happy group of children to school. But besides much joy, there will also be trouble once in a while. You can be glad they all come home for the noon meal with a hearty appetite and that you do not have to send the lunch with them as we here. School begins at nine, there is one hour free at noon, and at four school is over.

Ernest now goes happily with Willie to school each day. There is no school on Saturday, and now they have vacation until January 4. Tomorrow afternoon our church celebrates Christmas. Our pastor has two churches far apart.

How was business last summer? Was your work blessed with success? I do hope so. We all have reason to be grateful for our rich harvests, and we are all well again. I had two bad months, but I am better now but not as well as I should be.

Yesterday, on Christmas Day, I received a present which I enjoy from Uncle Alfred from Columbus, a pretty Christmas card and the pictures of Lina and Paul. They are charming, and I wish I could show them to you. Do you know tomorrow is my Rudolf's birthday? He would be sixteen years old now if he were still here. Oh, how I often yearn for him. Be calm, my soul; one day this longing will be fulfilled!

I can well believe how much you are interested in hearing from Mr. Bossard about here. Yes, one hears much more than from letters. I would be so glad if Brother Fritz would soon write me a long letter, but he must not forget the greetings to Mr. Bossard. If I myself should perhaps travel to Switzerland in the near future, would I also be welcome and find a place there? I would only need a little corner at night. During the daytime we could manage. Don't be cross with me, dear Anna, that I write so little. My thoughts are with you every day. My best wishes to your little baby Klara. So you will have someone at home when the others are at school. I am so much alone.

Best greetings to you all –

L. Ritter

Greetings from Mrs. Kunz to Mother. She sold her farm and will move to one of our places next spring. Lina's youngest is a three month old boy called Fritz. Do write soon. Greetings to whoever asks about me.

L. R.

[1]Luebke, *Immigrants and Politics,* p. 46.
[2]Brunner, *Immigrant Farmers and Their Children,* pp. 106-107.
[3]Luebke, p. 44.

INTRODUCTORY NOTE
For Letter of March 21, 1909

Life might have been easier for Louise if she had had a daughter. The Swiss mother and daughter had a special relationship. Between them were none of the rituals of a guest and a hostess. Each could enter the home of the other in the absence of the other. They frequently visited just for companionship and often worked together. A daughter would come to the mother for help in knitting or other projects. She would do house-cleaning and cooking for her parents when her mother was ill.[1] Louise had been cut off from this relationship with her own mother and had no daughter with whom to establish it.

Fritz had his sons, who shared his responsibilities and interests. There was no one to help Louise. When the boys were small, they helped her in the house; but when they were old enough, they helped with the farming. Her work load increased as the sons grew older. There was always the family to cook for as well as hired help in the harvest season. Fritz was not selfish about the money; she did have household conveniences, but it would have been less lonely if she had had someone to work beside her. Later, she hoped for daughters-in-law with whom this relationship could be developed.

Tilden, March 21, 1909

Beloved Mother,

Soon winter will be over; the sun is climbing higher and sending its rays down to earth so that it will soon be green. Easter will bless the sad human hearts with rich comfort and point to the eternal heavenly love and to the victory of life over death. The formidable snow drifts which the bad storms piled up high diminish from day to day in the milder weather. I would like to know how you, dear Mother, survived the winter, and how the girls from the dairy looked after you. They are growing up now. They are twelve, eleven, and ten years old; and Fritz will soon be seven. He will also go to school now. He would be a good playmate for our Ernest. He will go to school now. Our school closes this week already.[2]

I can't remember if I wrote you that Rosetti sold her farm and that she now lives on one of ours. There is only a small house there, but they get along all right. Why didn't they look around for something more suitable at the right time? Neighbors of ours are in town now. They have a large house with nine rooms. They have enough space but complain about boredom. They meant to auction their things, but the evening before a terrible snowstorm came as if all devils were let loose. You have never seen anything like it in Switzerland. Many people could not feed their animals that day, others only with great trouble. Many animals died buried in the snow and suffocated.

We already had a bad storm on January 28. The evening before all the families had to get their children from school. The storm was so violent that they could hardly see the road. In some places children froze to death. There were no houses to be seen, and there were drifts five to eight feet high. When the sun sends his warm rays down, the horror of the blizzard is forgotten. I have already planted some lettuce and will plant peas soon. They aren't killed by frost.

We have already sold forty head of cattle. Fred went with twenty to Omaha in February, and Hans with twenty the beginning of March. There are twenty still here. Soon they will plant the corn and grain. In the near future we want to build on two rooms and a pantry. Then I will have more work with cleaning them. I could do with some help – there is lots of work and food to be cooked.

Did you, dear Mother, stay a long time in Ins? How are they all? So Anna's Ernst is going to be confirmed at Easter. Fritz didn't keep his promise to write me soon. He doesn't care what we Americans do and how we are.

I hope to hear from you soon. Best greetings to all across the ocean. I am thinking of you always!
L. Ritter and Family

[1]Weinberg, *Peasant Wisdom,* pp. 63-64.
[2]"Sometimes these classes were held from September to February or November to March. School terms were not over 3 or 4 months." "History of Founding of Tilden," *Tilden Citizen,* 28 July 1955, p. 2.

INTRODUCTORY NOTE
For Letter of May 14, 1910

During this decade, world events disrupted the harmony that had been established in Louise's life. There are fewer letters during this decade and more time between them.

Fritz and the boys expanded their circle of activities. They went to Omaha and Chicago with the cattle they shipped, and the boys bought a car. In January of this year, Fritz was one of six members, including the pastor, to decide about the parsonage to be purchased for the church.

But Louise's life was centered around the home, a few friends, and the letters. Rarely did she attend the women's organization in the church.[1] After the record in 1903 of her contribution for the Communion Service, the next mention of her participation is as a guest on September 10, 1910. Her isolation made her dream of a visit by Bertha even more important. Bertha could have become her daughter.

Tilden, May 14, 1910

Beloved Mother,

I want to use this opportunity to send you a few lines through a friend. I have been waiting for news from you for a long time and am wondering if you are sick since you don't write. I hope good news will come soon.

I hope, dear Mother, you will welcome warmly the bringer of my letter. He is Mr. August Uhlmann from Emmen near Luzerne, and he kindly agreed to take my message to you when I asked him. I would have liked to travel with him, but we have so much work that I cannot get away at present.

How are you, dear Mother? And how are Anna and her family? Otto's[2] card from Ins pleased me much. I hope he will write more; he can do it very nicely. Many greetings to all in Ins. What are Bertha and those three doing? Ask Bertha if she would not like to come to America.[3] I would accept her as my child. Perhaps she could come with Mr. Uhlmann when he returns. She would like it here and soon would chatter in English. Our Willie and Ernest have school until the 20th.[4] Willie was sick last month. Ernest is stronger than he.

Hans was in Chicago with the fat cattle and saw a lot. The boys now have a car.[5] Fred drives very well. Ernest says that you should come here, Grandma, and you could ride in the car, too.

I'll enclose two pictures of our dear Rudolf, one for you, dear Mother, and one for Sister Anna. Our deceased ones live in spite of having died. I have to close; Mr. Uhlmann wants to leave.

Best greetings to all from
Louise Ritter and Family

[1]"Mother didn't get out much to learn English, and she never got away from home much. She did have some close friends." Interview, Ernest Ritter, January 1979.

[2]Otto is Anna's fourth son, age fourteen.

[3]Bertha, Emma's third daughter, is now eleven years old.

[4]The school term made a decided improvement in length. In the March 21, 1909 letter, Louise said the school closed the week of March 21.

[5]Their family was among the first in the area to own a car. Ernest does not remember in what year they bought the first one, but he remembers as a child waiting with the rest of the family for the older brothers to arrive with the car. They were not afraid of new machinery or new ideas. Interview, Ernest Ritter, December 1978.

INTRODUCTORY NOTE
For Letters of December 24, 1911, and January 1, 1912

One desire of immigrants was to gain prestige in their homeland and in the new land. Those in Switzerland knew of the Ritter family's success through Louise's letters, while Fritz's purchases of new machinery and the car indicated his success to the community. Fritz and Louise could now begin to take life easier. They planned to build a new house. The sons took over the farming and bought the land their father had made available for them. One evidence of their decision to enjoy life was the trip they took to the State Fair. This was the first trip Louise had taken since she had arrived in Nebraska. The others had traveled to Omaha and Chicago with the live stock they shipped.

She was excited about the new house, and enjoyed the trip. Far from clinging to her sons, she felt it was time for them to begin their lives. The two oldest were twenty-four and twenty-three years old.

Even in the midst of activity and excitement there was the undercurrent of sadness. Deaths and tragedies occurred on both sides of the ocean. Christmas was close to Rudolf's birthday and always a time for her to remember this lost son.

Tilden, December 24, 1911

Beloved Mother,

It is Christmas Eve, and I send you my best wishes for Christmas and the New Year.

Excuse me, dear Mother, for not writing for so long. I intended to do so, and Fritz urged me, too; but the time goes so fast, and I am rather negligent.

I don't know if you heard that Lina Strahm's little son died. He had a strange sickness. On May 3 he was wakened by his grandmother Rosetti after he had slept for hours, and from that time on he was unconscious until his death at noon, May 5. The doctor didn't know what caused it. He said that he was poisoned by a cold. They still have three girls; the little boy was two years and seven months old.

Last spring you told me of the death of Alex Schurch and of Mrs. Rudolf Schurch. Has Ruedi also died already? Please answer these questions for me in your next letter.

How is Cousin Fritz in Jegenstorf? It is hard for him and for Rosetti that he is sick so much. May he soon recover! Is Julia with them? How is it at your cheese plant? If I could only have Bertha!

Last October I had a letter from Aunt Lina in Columbus. She has had much sorrow because of her children. Lina was sick all spring, but fortunately has completely recovered. Last fall Paul was struck down, robbed and strangled by a Negro. Then Adele was sick, had to be operated on, and was in danger of death for a long time. She is home now. Aunt thought it would be spring before Adele would have her strength back. Aunt wrote that she had had a greeting from you, dear Mother, and she would enjoy receiving a letter from you. If it is not too much trouble, do write to her.

Last fall, Father and I went together with a few Tilden people to Lincoln to the State Fair. Oh, it was well worth it. In all that was exhibited each thing seemed to be better than the other. In the evening were grand fireworks, free theater, and concerts. We were there for three days.[1]

This winter Willie goes to the confirmation class,[2] and Ernest must go alone to his English school. Willie cannot go to the Christmas celebration since he has the measles. Ernest will get them too, probably. We have a Christmas tree in our house and one in church.

Best greetings to all,
Always your
Louise, Fritz and Children

Tilden, January 1, 1912

Dear Sister and Family,

My heartiest wishes for the New Year, may God bless you.

Yesterday, on New Year's Eve, I received your nice card, and on Christmas Day the one from your Alfred, that darling fellow. Many thanks for it. Did you and Grandmother receive my cards around Christmas? At dear Mother's it must have been very quiet during the holidays. I can believe, dear Sister, that you would have liked to have kept her longer. Thanks for that and also that you take such good care of her, and for all the good you do by visiting her and having her for a visit. I wish I could have her here and care for her. We would have enough room and food. As you said in your last letter, it really would be good if we lived closer together and could visit each other from time to time. It probably would be as it was with Fritz and me with Rosetti and Elise when we saw each other again after many years. We did not know one another very well at first, but after seeing each other several times that strangeness disappeared. Both have grown rather old. Elise is all white – do understand me – I mean her face. Her cheeks used to be red, but now she is always pale. Rosetti has to swallow a lot from her son-in-law. And the quick and unexpected death of her only grandson last May grieved her very much. I can understand that so well, as it happened to me. Dec. 27 Rudolf would have been nineteen years old, and Sept. 17, Fritz Strahm would have been four. May the Lord protect your children. I know very well, my dear Sister, if you had to lose one of your children, you would rather add more to your burden than to have an empty place at your table. We have to remember: "The

116

Lord gives, and He takes – the Lord's name be praised."

Deep snow covers the ground. This morning it was bitter cold, but we did go to church to attend the New Year's service. Driving the car is over now for the winter.[3] We finished harvesting the corn on Nov. 18. The garden vegetables like melons, cucumbers, and onions were quite good. Tomatoes were less good. I never had enough beans for a vegetable serving at a meal, just a soup bowl full once in a while. To our surprise, fruit and berries were good although in the spring frost threatened the blossoms. We had heaps of apples and made cider, five gallons of it. We also had plenty of cherries. I canned thirty-three quarts. The wild cherry trees were so covered with blossoms that one could not see the leaves. Their fruit grows like the currants in little clusters and are about their size with little stones. They make an excellent jelly and wine. We have to be grateful for all that grew last summer. The heat was often so intense that one felt like passing out, and it started very early. If it had rained enough, it wouldn't have been so bad. We had no good rains from spring to October. In October it rained more than through the whole summer.[4]

And now the latest which seems almost unbelievable: this spring we will have a new house built two miles out of town. Sand and bricks are already on the site. The two oldest sons will remain here and will run the farm. There does not seem to be the prospect of a young wife for either yet. We have had water in the house for a year. Fritz says that they will have gas lights in the house if or when one of them gets married. The central heating system works well. When you, dear Sister, come with your family to visit us, there will be plenty of room for all.

Oh, how I wish I could chat with you instead of sending my scribble. Dear Sister, please let my mother read this letter. She will be interested in several things. I never write two letters alike.[5]

[1]The program for the State Fair on September 7 and 8 included the following events: 5:00 p.m. – Wright Bros. in flight from the center field at the race track. 6:45 p.m – Program by Liberati before the grand stand. Music between acts by the Ferranti Royal Italian Guards Band and the Hebron Band. Stupendous display of fireworks. 10:30 a.m. – Liberati's Concert Band and Grand Opera Company at the Auditorium. *Lincoln Daily Star*, 7 September 1911, p. 1.

It was Nebraska's forty-third annual state fair, and "the biggest fair the state has ever seen, every department having made big increases since last year." *Lincoln Daily Star*, 4 September 1911, pp. 1, 2.

"The attendance Monday was 20,213 or nearly 7,000 more than on Monday of last year which broke all previous records." *Lincoln Daily Star*, 5 September 1911, p. 1.

[2]Confirmation instruction was in German and taught by their minister.

[3]During the winter, the car was put up on blocks and they drove horses again. Interview, Ernest Ritter, December 1978.

[4]The rainfall cycle for the years 1910 to 1920 is recorded as irregular. Most years were dry. Olson, *History of Nebraska*, p. 13. A more general reference reports local drought conditions were experienced from 1910 to 1915. Lawson, Dewey, Neild, *Climatic Atlas of Nebraska*, p. 55.

117

[5]This is significant since she had been writing letters for eighteen years, never having seen one of them in that time. The closest she came was sending messages with someone visiting them.

Theodore Blegen calls the letters of immigrants to their European family and friends the common people's diary. These letters are of interest to modern readers because the contemporary recorders were personally experiencing a change of worlds.[1] Their letters documented the events and changes. The pardonable pride Louise expressed in their "village" indicated they had left their "dog days" of frontier life behind. Now, she anticipated daughters-in-law who might live with her.

The next world the family would experience is foreshadowed in her concern for world affairs. As Germany became more aggressive, and public opinions formed, she would become an outsider again. In Europe, the community provided the basis for personality and self respect; but here the familiar, especially language, was to become an occasion for threats and humiliation.[2]

Tilden, May 10, 1912

Beloved Mother,

Your card and letter are in my hands now; so after long waiting I have a token of life from my homeland. I had thought the letter had sunk with the unfortunate *Titanic*.

I am so glad that you are well and that all at Sister Anna's are well. But I am deeply sorry that Anna, that poor child, has to work although she doesn't wish to. That does not bring happiness and contentment, rather the opposite. How can I do anything from this distance when you cannot do anything being so near? Perhaps things have changed in the meantime – I hope so from the bottom of my heart.

So, on Easter, Anna Konig, Otto Wuthrich, and Willie Ritter will all be confirmed – one child of each of the sisters. Our pastor thinks we should send Willie to the seminary in St. Louis, but Willie does not want it, so he will most likely become a farmer with God's help.

On June 3, they began to build our new home. The basement was dug and walled in May. Now the floors have to be cemented in the basement so that mice and rats cannot come in. There will be central heating and perhaps gas lights.[3] Also there will be water in the house, just like here. There will be room for a daughter-in-law, or even for two. Our house is the nicest and largest in the neighborhood. It has eight large, bright rooms, a pantry, bathroom, four large closets, and outside cemented sidewalks. Next to it is the large wash house with a power washer and room for fire wood.[4] Further back is the new, large horse barn with room for eighteen horses and a bin for

119

storing oats. Above the horse stalls, I think ten to twelve feet high, there is room for hay and straw, and on the very top an elevator for unloading the hay. Other buildings provide storage space for corn and grain, corn on the cob, and shelter for hogs and cattle. There is a garage and a chicken house. It is a real little village. We have eighteen horses, twelve of them four and five years old.

July 14. Is it possible that I began this letter two months ago? The hot and busy time passed so quickly. Now we are in the midst of summer. In the middle of May we had a good rain and had cool weather up to the end of May. Now it is very hot, and we have had no rain. Last week a thunder storm brought us two inches of refreshing rain. But now all is wilted again – may God send us some rain soon.

Before these lines reach you, the harvest will have begun. It does not look very good. If we get more rain in time, the corn can still be good, and that is our main crop. The gardens need rain badly. There are no apples on the trees. I canned more than forty quarts of cherries and eight quarts of strawberries. All kinds of berries are plentiful. Hans's vineyard looks good. Hans is a good farmer. Fred is an automobile agent and Willie an agent for a Chicago medicine firm. Ernest can help me a lot, bring in the fire wood, feed the chickens, etc. The two agents need not travel about with their merchandise. Fred sold three cars, but one of them he could not get from the factory.

July 23. Again an interruption. We are in the midst of harvesting. There is not much wheat and oats because of the drought. Yesterday and today it was very hot again; last week it was cool and rainy. Yesterday afternoon, Father, I, and Ernest went to town. At night there was a storm with a good rain, and it looks as if there will be more rain. It is so humid and cloudy. We harvested some potatoes already.

Tilden, August 1912

Beloved Sister and Family,

How negligent I am with writing; it shouldn't be like that! Please, dear Sister, forgive me, but you write often and let your girls write soon to their American aunt, or your dear boys if the girls are too busy.

Today is such a beautiful, quiet Sunday. We were at church in the morning. We attend it regularly. We like our church! Last week we had such a good rain, and everything looks so fresh after being dry for some time. The grain was only fair, if only the corn continues to grow well nothing will be lost.

I think of you so often because you are always so uncertain in your business. It would be good if your prices at your dairy were high as the prices are everywhere.[5] If there should be a set back? Oh, I dare not think of it; I am so afraid. Do come to America and become free. Bring our dear mother along.

There are elderly people like her here. Only this morning I visited a family in town where the father and mother are eighty-three, and we know others that age. So pack and come! But on the side, dear Sister, as soon as your daughter is grown up have her learn sewing. How often I have regretted not having learned it. I can sew just everyday dresses, but I don't dare to try to sew Sunday dresses. To have them made is expensive here. One can order ready-made dresses which fit quite well or need only a little alteration. I do think you should think seriously about emigration and – come. The chapters which I would have to endure in various paragraphs and verses after your emigration, ha, ha, ha – I will bear and try to digest.

September 9. I had not really expected that there would be such a long delay with this letter. Since Aug. 17, we have had a terrible heat and only one hour of rain. The corn has suffered badly from the hot winds, but we hope that we shall have enough to get us through another year.

Our house is finished now. The outside is white and is going to have a yellow trim. As soon as I have a picture of the house, I'll send you one. Perhaps we can move in by the end of the month. The longer we stay here, the more Fred and Hans like it. They still don't have any plans for wives. Ernest begins school today, and Willie will go to school after the corn is picked. Young people can go to school until they are twenty-one years old but can stop earlier. If only your Anna were here (you others as well) perhaps she could cook for her cousins.

Is it really true that the weather in Switzerland is so bad that the grain and potatoes are spoiled because of the rains? We seem to have exchanged sun and rain between us. We have not had bad thunder storms, but in Chicago there was such a terrible one that it reduced forty buildings and blocks to ruins. I hope it is not bad with you; papers often exaggerate.

And won't the Italians soon stop fighting?[6] We heard they had plans for taking Switzerland. The Emperor Wilhelm would probably come to help. Did any of you see him? I would think the Swiss would be proud of welcoming such a high guest, or would they not? I'll come back to the Italians; does this unfortunate war affect you all? Oh, I think war is a horror; just think of those many innocent people who are drawn into it. May God preserve us from that evil.

How is our good mother? Do none of Emma's children sleep with her? I hope that one is always with her. Is Anna now in the seminary?[7] I would like to hear something of Rosetti Basch. These are many questions all at once, aren't they? And when one finally gets to answering, all are mostly forgotten. I hope you are all well and will write a long, good letter to me soon. Your children are still having a vacation and write in German (naturally) which my children can't, and you can't read English.

Best greetings and wishes to a successful business year.
Louise Ritter

[1]Blegen, *Land of Their Choice,* pp. 144-145.

[2]Bernard, *Americanization Studies,* pp. 47-48.

[3]Gas lights were installed in the new house. They were carbide lights. The carbide came in 100 gallon drums, was buried, and flooded with water. When the carbide was no longer effective, the water had to be drained. But the lights were convenient. They were located throughout the house and turned on by the pull of a chain which struck the flint to give the spark. Hot plates could be operated by this system also. Interview, Ernest Ritter, January 1979.

[4]Louise's washing was done with a tub and wash board the first years. Then she had a hand pump machine. With the wash house came an engine and power shaft to do the washing. Interview, Ernest Ritter, January 1979.

[5]In Europe capital exports had "begun to loom large in all countries that had money to invest," and it "caused some branches of domestic economies to suffer because of high interest." Herbert Heaton, *Economic History of Europe,* rev. ed. (New York: Harper & Row, Pub., 1948), pp. 668-669.

[6]The Italians had had a long period of unrest, internal strikes, and political tensions. They had trouble with Austria because of her persecutions of her Italian subjects. In November of 1911, Italy clashed with Turkey and France when she took Liberia in Africa. Donald Kagan, et al, *The Western Heritage Since 1648* (New York: Macmillan Publishing Co., Inc., 1979), pp. 815-817.

[7]It is not clear which sister's daughter this is; both had an Anna. Neither is there any information on the "seminary."

Since Louise wrote more often about her rheumatism, it is easy to visualize her as an old woman and forget that she was only fifty years old at the time these letters were written. Immigration, the "dog days," and grief had aged her beyond the chronological years.

The letters show her increasing concern about the unsettled world situation. A Swiss's strong sense of family is not limited to immediate household members. It extends to vast numbers of cousins, no matter how remote. She feared for the safety of those in Europe, and in spite of their protests, renewed her appeal that they come to join them in Nebraska and be safe. She would have liked all of the family in Nebraska where she could have looked after their welfare; and, of course, she would have had company.

Tilden, January 1, 1913

Beloved Mother,

I received your and Aunt Julia's letters on Christmas Day. Thanks for all the good wishes. I also hope that you celebrated a Merry Christmas and a Happy New Year's Day. For the new year I wish you good health, happiness and God's blessings, and to both you and Aunt Julia a healing of your pains and sicknesses. Dear Mother, I wonder where you were over the holidays – in Iffwyl or in Ins. I do hope that Aunt Julia feels better and that you stay with Sister Anna and her family. Aunt Julia must not think that there is no rheumatism in America. She is much mistaken in that idea. There is too much here. I have it also, especially in my feet, and I have to walk as on eggs. You can imagine how long the days are for me since I have to walk so carefully. I can only stand and walk with great pain. Just now at this time it is not too bad, except when I am baking for the holidays.[1] Willie and Ernest[2] are good dishwashers, and they can dry the dishes, sweep and wash the floors.

As you know, dear Mother, Willie was confirmed last spring. For a time he did not attend the English school so that he would not get too mixed up with everything. Now he can catch up with his work at the English school since he has the time. Boys and girls can have school free until their twenty-first year. Willie grew a lot last summer; he is taller than I. He was healthier than usual as he worked a lot in the fields. He often said he could jump into the air because he was so happy that he did not have to go to the pastor for lessons. This gentleman had only five boys and one girl in his class, but he was often very angry for nothing. He does not like children, and they don't like him. Dear, dignified Papa Ziegler in Messen was a teacher for the young who deserved to be presented as an example for the others. I also remember with affection my teacher Mr. Andreas Sutter. These two were more faithful in the Lord and may God bless them. I sent greetings to him through my aunt, and now my mother tells me of his death. I think for him it was a happy homecoming. His home was in a better world where many have already gone before him. Let us also with believing, happy hearts look up to heaven where we will be reunited with our beloved ones who hurried there before us.

I am so glad to hear that Cousin Rosetti is well again. Please give her and Elise and their families my best greetings.

I am sorry that you don't want to hear anything about emigrating here, but perhaps it still can happen. When it gets so restless, you would be safer here. In Europe, it is like a powder magazine,[3] and I worry about you all the time. May the Lord turn all dangers away from Switzerland and from all who are close and dear to me.

We are now living in our new home, and Fred and Hans are masters in the other place alone. I bake and wash for them; and if God makes me well again, I will do as much as I can for them. They often come to us, and I am so happy about this because they are such good sons. I wish them both the best for their future. If they had a housekeeper or if one would marry a pious virgin, I would be happy. Let's hope for the best. Our new home is very nice. We have central heating and gas lights. But the water is not in yet and we miss it very much. It was too late in the fall to put it in, so we have to be patient until spring.

So far the weather has been very nice and mild, but it can easily change. And are you having such a hard winter? Can you protect yourself enough from the cold? Aren't any of Emma's girls with you? At least overnight? If they were, it would be comforting for me. The children from the cheese plant will have grown quite a bit since their picture was taken. Many thanks for it. They should not be angry with me anymore. I meant to write and hope I'll do it one day. Yes, if I had a daughter as you have three, I would most likely have more time for writing. Why don't the girls write to me? I would be so glad. Where is Anna now? Greetings and best wishes to all. I'll write soon.

Dear Mother, stay well and write soon. Many thousand greetings from all of us.

Your Louise Ritter and Family

Tilden, January 5, 1913

Beloved Sister and Family,

Happy New Year to you all; good health and to your father a prosperous business.

Dear Sister, I meant to wait for your letter so that I could answer it immediately. You will have received my card in the meantime. Since I have

124

not heard from you yet, I don't want to wait any longer! Did dear Mother spend the holidays with you or did Aunt Julia get worse? I hope she was with you or is still there. Surely everyone enjoys it when Grandma comes for a visit. We have to get along without her.

You don't want to hear any more about coming to America – perhaps you'll change your mind one day. I can understand Mother; she is afraid of the long voyage. We are not cross with you; we don't want to force anyone. But it does not seem so secure anymore in Switzerland. Why and with whom do you good Swiss people take sides? It is much better to put the sword away. Come to America; it is a good life under the flag of the stars. There are already many here from Fritz's side of the family, but none from mine.

Yesterday, Jan. 4, it snowed, and today it is stormy and bitter cold so Hans and Fred could not come to us. We moved here the beginning of December, and now the two big sons have to keep house alone until one gets married. I wish it were soon because I can't work so well anymore. From March to August last year I had a sore toe and could hardly walk. Since I got over that, rheumatism has taken over, and walking and standing are very painful as the pain is in the legs and feet. One always has to be plagued by something so that the world is not too dear. There are many here with rheumatism.

Now we are only a half hour away from town; it used to be a full hour. Our address is the same since we are on the same route. How I wish that you could all visit us here! What a joy it would be, believe me, and I won't give up hope.

Before Christmas I received a letter from Aunt Lina in Columbus, Ohio. She is very worried about Paul, who has been sick for a long time. He went from one sanitorium to the other all through the summer. He and Aunt Lina spent six weeks with relatives in the country this fall. When they returned, Paul thought he could work again; but the old trouble started again. Now the old mother has to take care of her grown-up son instead of the other way around. Aunt writes that since he was attacked, strangled, and robbed by a Negro two years ago, he has never been quite the same. When the girls and Paul were here, the girls could not get over how much Paul smoked all the time. It would be all right if that were good for a young person. I always say that in large cities are too many temptations for young people. They can be well brought up at home and still be led away from these teachings. Poor Aunt! Don't say anything to her.

What do your children do and learn? Is Ernst now a mechanic? Soon the girls will grow up. You know what? Anna could come here and keep house for my boys, or perhaps Martha. Emma and Klara would prefer to stay with their mother, I am sure, and play with their dolls they received for Christmas. What does Alfred do? Is he busily going to school and learning eagerly, so that he will be a fine man like his father? I was sorry to hear that your business has gone down; the expected setback has already come. The farmers

125

ought to go down with their milk prices. Don't lose your courage. There will be a place for you in the new year.

Dear Sister, you have your own sewing machine, haven't you? My husband gave me a Damascus for the new year. I will have to try it soon.

January 7. The machine does not run easily; perhaps it will get better. I can use it a few days, and if I am not satisfied we can send it back. Yesterday, I hoped to receive a letter from you, but in vain. Perhaps you are prevented from writing, or did your letter get lost? Do write soon! I do hope you all and Mother are well. If only I could travel with my letter! But it is now just a bit too cold to travel.

Best greetings from all of us. Happy birthday to Mother. I wrote to her a week ago.

Your Louise and Family

[1]For the holiday season she baked special breads, meringues, and a deep fat fried pastry translated into "knee patches." A braided bread was a tradition for New Year's Day. Interview, Ernest Ritter, December 1978.

[2]Willie was now almost seventeen, and Ernest was eleven and a half years old.

[3]Events in Europe included the First Balkan War starting in 1912, the Italian-Turkish War which ended in 1912, and the clash between Germany and France over Morocco. Stewart C. Easton, *The Western Heritage,* 2nd ed. (New York: Holt, Rinehart and Winston, Inc., 1966), p. 704.

The earlier letters of 1913 dealt with Louise's concern over the unsettled world situation. In the first of these letters, she recounted the tragic effects of violent weather. Her concern was not confined to the state, but included Ohio, where her kinfolk were endangered by flooding. Of greater concern to her was that she could do no more to help these family members in time of grief than she had been able to help those back in Switzerland.

The pain of separation is a theme found throughout the letters. Death, failure of communication, changing attitudes, aging – all of these were threats to the solidarity of the family. Letters were infrequent. She asked, "Didn't you and the Konig family receive my letter last spring? It is ages since I have heard from you." It would have been easier for her to maintain family solidarity if she had had some help. "If only someone of my relatives would come here." She was tired.

Tilden, June 18, 1913

Beloved Mother,

I received your letter more than two weeks ago, and I am glad that you are well again. I would like to thank those good people, Fritz and Marie, personally for what they did for you.[1] But that is not easy now as I am not fit for traveling. My condition has not yet improved; often I think it is almost worse.

We had such a nice January and February that March and April must have thought they had to do what the previous month neglected doing. They really exchanged their roles. March 1 began with a bad blizzard, then March 15 brought another which was even worse. The cattlemen west of us had terrible losses, and in the prairies they lost 20 to 40 cattle and more per owner. Many went bankrupt. The animals which were outside ran with the storm until they fell into a river or a ravine. Soon they were covered with snow and suffocated. Yes, March 1913 will remain a bitter memory with many people all their lives.[2]

On Easter Sunday at 6:00 p.m., the sky in the southeast turned red in a frightening way, and there was lightning and thunder. And then it happened. In Omaha death and destruction came. It was horrible. Hans was there shortly afterwards, and he said that it looked terrible even though they had already cleared away much of the damage. First, it was said that there were 500 deaths in Omaha, and it was a miracle that there were only 200, and perhaps three times that number injured. There was deep mourning in many families, and it was heart-breaking to see a picture of a family of seven who were all killed.[3]

127

Shortly after Easter, I wrote to Aunt Lina in Columbus. You may have heard that the floods were at their worst the week after Easter. I worried about her as the east of that town was badly damaged. After a long time I received an album of pictures of the area so badly damaged there, but not one written word. Do you know anything of those poor people? Apparently not, according to your and Anna's letter of last week. April 28 I received a telegram saying, "Paul died yesterday, funeral on Wednesday (30th)," I wrote to them but so far no answer. It is so hard on Aunt, first to lose her husband and now her only son. How is Aunt Julia? Greetings to Rosetti and Elise and also to Aunt Julia. Is she in Messen again?

Greetings to all, and remain well, write soon,

L. Ritter

Tilden, December 17, 1913

Beloved Mother,

The year hurries to its end and with God's will we will enter the new year. We have seen just recently how little time it often takes to take a person away from this earth. A young mother was called away in the town in the early morning in a few minutes, leaving her husband with four little children.

Our aunt in Columbus still cannot accept it that Paul is gone, and yet the poor man was released from his long suffering. I still don't know what his illness was. I had a letter from Aunt Lina in November, but she could not make herself write about it. It is hard for her to lose father and son in such a short time. Aunt would have liked to have given Julia a present each year, but her expenses were too much so she cannot do it now. I hope things will soon be better for the three women. Anna still has the same job, and Lina has over fifty pupils in her school, and she loves it.

The news from Ins tells me that you, dear Mother, are well, and I am so glad. Didn't you and the Konig family receive my letter last spring? It is ages since I have heard from you. I hope things are well in the dairy business. Greetings to all. Is Fritz now going alone to school? If only someone of my relatives would come here; perhaps Emma's girls or one of Anna's sons. Walter[4] is so curious about America; he should come here for a few years. That would be something new for him. One need not be afraid of Indians or wild animals here. At night we sleep as peacefully as you in dear Switzerland. Is the young Fritz Kunz of Mulchi still in South America?[5]

Our two big sons have been living alone now for more than a year. I wish they would bring home nice wives. All that time I have washed, baked, and mended for them. It is hard for me because of my arthritis. When I planted the garden, I could not use my left hand. I could not reach the ground so I had to use my shoe. Who knows what the winter will bring. I will trust the Lord

128

that He will help us all through our troubles. Willie and Ernest are busy with their school. The day after tomorrow they will have a Christmas tree at the school, and afterwards they will have two weeks of vacation. School began in Sept. and lasts nine months. Then Ernest still has German lessons for two months with our pastor.[6] He has been very satisfied with him. He has praised him on how well he can read, better than others who have had four to five years of lessons.

We are having wonderful weather for this time of year.

Excuse me for closing my letter already. Otherwise, it might get too heavy. I'll enclose a dollar hoping you will buy something with it for the new year, perhaps a good bottle of wine.

Best greetings from all. We wish you a mild winter and prosperity with your cheese factory. Happiness and health.

Your ever,

Fritz, Louise Ritter and Sons

[1]Emma's husband, Fritz Konig, remarried. He and his second wife, Marie, maintained close ties with Anna and Louise's mother.

[2]"North Platte, Neb. March 24 – Not since the winter of 1880-1881 have stockmen in this locality suffered such a loss to cattle from storm. It is estimated that no less than 1,000 head of cattle were lost in this county alone. Some of the cattlemen lost 50 percent of their herds ... The *North Platte Tribune* estimates the loss to cattlemen in territory tributary to North Platte at $150,000. The greatest losses were from cattle driven ahead of the storm into the rivers and lakes." "Territory of North Platte Badly Hurt by Losses of Stock," *Oakdale Sentinel,* 28 March 1913, p. 6.

[3]"Between 140 and 200 killed, twice that number badly injured and hundreds of thousands of dollars worth of property destroyed, briefly tell the story of the tornado which swept throughout Omaha and its suburbs at 6 o'clock Sunday evening in an almost straight pathway four to six miles long .... The villages of Benson, Dundee, and Florence, suburbs of Omaha, were practically wiped out." "200 Are Dead and 400 Injured in Cyclone and Fire at Omaha," *Oakdale Sentinel,* 13 March 1913, p. 7.

[4]Walter, Anna's third son, was eighteen years old – a good age for a trip to America. But he never came.

[5]Swiss not only came to the United States. From 1884 to 1941 there were 20,522 who went to Brazil and from 1857 to 1926, 38,000 went to Argentina. Bernard, Zeleny, and Miller, *American Immigration Policy,* pp. 223-224.

[6]Willie's German lessons were cut short because the pastor left. Ernest attended long enough so he could read and write German. Of course, he could speak it since he grew up speaking both English and Swiss-German.

INTRODUCTORY NOTE
For Letters of April 2 and November 21, 1915

There are no letters for the year of 1914. If Louise had been concerned for her family before, she had further reason once the war broke out. The European power struggles of the second half of the Nineteenth century had produced a change in the Swiss situation. The Swiss were completely encircled by big powers, like no other small nation in the world. It was a perilous situation in view of the rivalries between France and Germany, Austria and Italy. There is no need to review the events that led to the outbreak of the war. The outbreak of the war was a great blow to the hopes and ideals of the neutral Swiss. The Federal Council was determined to demonstrate that Swiss neutrality would be defended. On August 3 an army of nearly 250,000 men was mobilized.[1] One third of all of Switzerland's imports enter through the Rhine. Theoretically, of course, Germany was bound by the Treaty of Paris (1814) to keep the river open to navigation at all times; but in 1914, when the World War started, the treaty provisions were promptly ignored.[2] Economically, the war had found Switzerland ill prepared. In August 1914, the country had only a few weeks' bread supply, and after that the imports and exports by which they lived were at the mercy of the belligerent powers.[3] Because they were dependent on foreign countries for supplies of foodstuffs, the war was a period of trial for the Swiss from the economic, political, and moral point of view. They intended to maintain neutrality, but were caught in the middle. The Allies refused to supply foodstuffs unless Switzerland ceased to trade with Germany, while Germany threatened, if Switzerland did so, to withhold the necessary coal supplies. During the war years, the Swiss were completely dependent in their communications and trade with the outside world on railroads of neighboring countries which were already too busy because of their own wartime requirements. This resulted in a threat of famine which was averted by France and the United States. France kept a port open, and the United States provided grain and other supplies.[4]

It was not long before the effects were felt in Louise's other home, Nebraska. The first effects of the World War upon Nebraska were a sharp falling of the prices of grain and meat, accompanied by a financial depression which swept the nation. Exports to Europe were immediately cut-off by the declaration of war. A little later, as the war went on and the millions of European peoples were taken from the farms and factories for the war, there arose a great and growing demand for all the products of America, including food.[5]

The war had other effects on the immigrants, and ended with a change in the United States's policy towards immigration. Nearly all of the thirteen million foreign-born people in the United States were from countries now engaged in combat with one another; and a further nineteen million Americans were the children of European immigrants. When Wilson appealed to Americans in 1914 to be neutral in thought as well as in action, he could hardly have expected that his advice would be followed literally. In fact, the war was to show Old World ties were still remarkably influential; for most immigrant groups these ties now influenced political action.[6]

Louise was neutral and hoped only for peace. It was not until years later that she said anything about the persecution German-speaking people encountered, and then very little.

Tilden, April 2, 1915

Dear Sister and Family,

Today is Good Friday, a sunny still day with fresh spring air and even some birds singing. In the morning we went to a communion service.

The world around us does not look much like spring. There are still too many traces of winter; snow drifts are still two to three feet high, even more in some places. The sun has shone brightly the last few days, but in the mornings the windows are still frosted. During the day the roads are muddy. But spring will and must come. Since Christmas we have had so much snow that we were hardly able to get through it. Dear Sister, you will think that if we have no greater worries we should be satisfied, and that we will be. We trust in the Lord, and nothing will happen without His will that is not good for us. Don't let us forget that.

One would rather not look into the papers since there is nothing but quarrels, bad prophesies, and bloodshed all over the world. We hear hardly anything about Switzerland. Are you buying milk again? How did it go with your cheese trade?

Oh, how I ask myself daily how you are, and I cannot get any answer. I received your letter of February 1, and I am sorry I am answering it this late. Fritz got sick the middle of February and could not work. He must still be very careful not to get sick again.

Of course, we still have our farm with four horses, forty-five cattle, seventy-six hogs, over one hundred chickens, four cats (soon it will be two dozen!) and innumerable mice and rats. Now don't forget it again. By the way, you can come and convince yourselves of it. I would feel so much easier if I had you all with Mother here. Perhaps you may still come. It would be especially useful if one or rather two of the girls would learn to sew.

Is dear Mother with you now? And how is she? Is your son Ernst in uniform at the border?[7] Of course, we wish and hope that our dear Switzerland will not have war on its land. God may see to that.

Newspapers had the rumor that Italy would be involved in the war also, but that was later denied. They had better stay out of it. Every country would be wise to keep peace within their own borders and continue to grow. If only peace would come soon again among the people – to change swords to plows again and to feed the hungry.

April 5. Yesterday was Easter with bright sunshine. But soon it clouded over and started to rain. Spring is now really coming; the snow is disappearing rapidly. That is good because the farmers have to start with their field work as soon as the roads are less muddy. Many had trouble for months feeding the livestock.

The battling nations would do better to yield their land instead of hating each other. Even the Swiss government bought a lot of horses here.[8]

I may get reprimanded again because of the Emmenthal paper.[9] May it be; those who had to go through such hard times as we old pioneers have learned to honor the smallest thing. You may have to learn that yet. This is not meant to be nasty, but everyone has to make his own experiences and we have them.

I wish you all the very best and would like to save you from danger – if only I could!

Best greetings to all,
Louise Ritter and Family

Tilden, November 21, 1915

Beloved Niece,

I enjoyed your letter very much. I would have liked to have answered it immediately; the spirit was willing but the flesh was weak, as was true so often before. Didn't your mother write to us once all summer? I didn't receive any answers. In these uncertain times letters can easily be lost. Millions of people are pleading for peace, not only in Europe but also here in America and the whole world. Is your brother Ernst at the border again? How those poor people have to suffer because of this horrible war, especially those in the fighting lines. May the dear Lord protect our dear Switzerland from the evils of war. Can you earn some money in these times? I hope you, your mother, and grandmother will find time to write soon. We don't hear anything about how you are; may it not be too bad. We learned that they still build railroads. Are the summer cheeses sold and the milk trade settled for next year? How are the grandmothers in Iffwyl and the Konig family? I know these are too many questions at once, but I would be happy if you would answer them.

Now you children will all go to school again and study so that you will grow up to be capable people. We have only one pupil left. Ernest is very busy this winter. The school started the last Monday in August. He also goes to confirmation at the church and learns German there. Last spring, he took the exam for high school. There they study English, Latin, and algebra, in addition to other subjects. Ernest maintains that he will go there only one year – there are four years. No one can tell him if he should learn a trade; that is up to him. How nice it would be if your children and mine could get to know each other and visit together. It would be even better if you would come to America. How about that, dear niece? Wouldn't you like that? Of course, it is here as everywhere; not all that glitters is gold. But we must not complain. As long as we can live in peace, we will be content.

War taxes have been collected for months here. The cotton industry in the South has suffered since the beginning of the war. Others profit from it. It is said that hard times are before us. Wheat is one-third lower than the year before. Hogs have gone down two dollars per 100 lb. in three and four weeks. If a farmer has sixty to two hundred hogs and fed them with expensive corn, it is very bad for him with such low prices. No one knows about the cattle market, but everyone knows the high price they must pay to get cattle. Last spring they didn't make any money in the cattle market. This fall the farmers had to try hard to buy enough cattle and hogs to feed the corn which did not ripen. The weather was too cold and wet and the corn could not be brought to the market.

[1]Georg Thurer, *Free and Swiss,* trans. R.C. Heller and E. Long (London: Oswald Wolff, 1970), p. 142.

[2]Ronald Stuart Kain, *Europe: Versailles to Warsaw,* (New York: The H.W. Wilson Co., 1939), p. 332.

[3]Thurer, p. 146.

[4]Kain, pp. 332-333.

[5]Sheldon, *Nebraska,* I, p. 901.

[6]Jones, *American Immigration,* p. 140.

[7]There was and still is universal military training in Switzerland. Each soldier owns his own rifle and takes it home with him. As stated before, the Swiss army had been mobilized on the borders.

[8]Horse breeding was practiced on a grand scale in Switzerland, and she provided the cavalry of several European armies with mounts. Martin, *Switzerland,* p. 133.

[9]No information has been found concerning the reprimand.

There are no letters for the years 1916, 1917, and 1918. During these years the war in Europe affected most lives. After the sinking of *The Lusitania* in May of 1915, the anti-German attitudes began to become ugly in the United States. The American people never did really find out what was going on, nor did the people in other countries. American newsmen had not expected the war to occur and found themselves off guard. They were unable to assess calmly the events which were happening so rapidly. Their previous lack of attention to European affairs meant they knew little beyond what the government told them of the immediate crisis.[1] Headlines such as these in the local papers helped to whip up fear of German speaking people: "Call on Germans to Blast Plants. St. Louis Germans asked to bomb certain R. R. etc. to help homelands. Rewards offered."[2] The propaganda omitted mention of loyal Germans or good actions by German-Americans, so these people were made to appear unregenerate.[3]

When emotions run high, people can forget past friendships and self-righteously turn on the very people they knew as friends and neighbors before. Exalted patriots, thoroughly infected by the intolerant spirit of 100 percent Americanism, proclaimed that loyalty demanded the complete eradication of German culture. Accordingly, the teaching of German was in many places prohibited, and German music and opera were shunned. Towns, streets, and buildings with German names were rechristened; even sauerkraut became liberty cabbage, while hamburgers were renamed Salisbury steaks.[4]

The Smith-Towner Act, passed by Congress in 1918 at the request of the National Education Association, provided that no state could share in federal funds unless it enacted and enforced laws requiring that English was the chief language of instruction in all schools, both public and private. Early in 1919 fifteen states responded and seven went beyond the requirements and prohibited all instruction in German up to and including the eighth grade.[5] In Nebraska in 1918 the legislature repealed the Mockett Act of 1913, which required schools to give instruction in a foreign language if petitioned by fifty parents. In 1919 they enacted a law that forbade teaching of or in a foreign language in any school below the high school level. Robert T. Meyer, a teacher in a Lutheran parochial school in Hampton, Nebraska, violated this law. The case was appealed to the United States Supreme Court, and the law was ruled unconstitutional in 1923.[6]

Nebraskans also demonstrated their war hysteria by establishing 15,000 home guards in two hundred towns and Protective Leagues of amateur detectives. Card index lists were kept that indicated people's ability to contribute to the war effort by buying Liberty Bonds. "Slackers' lists" were compiled, and yellow paint was splashed on the houses of those suspected of being pro-German.[7] The Lutheran Church refused to buy or push Liberty Bond sales since this would have been a violation of conscience and principles of separation of church and state. In Riverdale, Nebraska, a crowd of patriots hanged an effigy before the parsonage of the local German Lutheran church; and in Papillion, Nebraska, the Rev. H.J. Schmidt was attacked and beaten.[8]

Tilden was caught in the same hysteria. The self-styled patriots did not distinguish between Germans and Swiss which was in itself an affront to the pride of the Swiss-Americans. The Ritter family had few problems; they just bought the Liberty Bonds assigned as their quota.[9] But some families were not that lucky. Two men in Tilden had their homes splashed with yellow paint and were periodically taken down to the main street to salute the Kaiser hanged in effigy. All the German books in the high school were taken out and burned. Mrs. Friedli, Fritz's sister, knit for the Red Cross until she was accused of putting crushed glass in the socks she knitted. Fortunately, most people recognized the ridiculousness of the charge.[10]

The German Evangelical Synod was especially sensitive about its origins which were tied to the creation of the Prussian State Church in 1817. They pointed out that the American church had never had any link with the German government.[11] The local Evangelical Friedens Church in Tilden suffered. The church minutes of January 17, 1914, state "an interesting and lively discussion was held, and it was decided to introduce the English language into Sunday School and leave it to the discretion of the pastor to use the English language in his duties as well as in instructions whenever the need arises." The war accelerated the language transition in the Evangelical Synod. Because their minister those years was definitely pro-German, he was frequently subjected to harrassment. One time when he visited the Ritter farm, his tires were slashed.[12] After the war he returned to Germany.

It would take many years before the wounds of the war would be healed. Europe had been devastated. Switzerland had been exhausted by privations. The United States had been disillusioned. Many communities had been divided by ethnic and language differences.[13]

[1]H.C. Peterson, *Propaganda for War* (Norman: University of Oklahoma Press, 1939), p. 160.

[2]*Oakdale Sentinel,* 3 September 1915, p. 3.

[3]Peterson, pp. 69-70.

[4]Jones, *American Immigration,* p. 271.

[5]Frederick C. Luebke, *Bonds of Loyalty* (DeKalb: Northern University Press, 1974), p. 312.

[6]Ibid., p. 313.

[7]Sheldon, *Nebraska,* I, p. 5.

[8]Luebke, *Bonds of Loyalty,* p. 280.
[9]Interview, Ernest Ritter, January 1979.
[10]Interview, Mrs. Olga Ritter, January 1979.
[11]Luebke, *Bonds of Loyalty,* p. 290.
[12]Interview, Ernest Ritter, December 1978.
[13]Copies of the *Tilden Citizen* for the war years are not available in microfilm nor at the local office.

Fritz and Louise

137

The Ritter sons. Back row Hans, Willie; front Ernest, Fred.

None of Louise's sons were in the war, but by the time this letter was written, many changes had occurred in the family. The three oldest sons were married, and Fritz and Louise's first grandchild had been born.

Some things had not changed; Louise still expressed hope that someone of her family would come to Nebraska. Also, she continued to report on the weather and crops. She continued to trust in God's will.

Tilden, December 30, 1919

Dear Mother, Dear Sister, Dear Niece Martha, and all other relatives in the whole house:

Yesterday I received your letter, and I want to answer it immediately. I hope you all celebrated Christmas in good health, and I hope that you, dear Mother, are well again. Our Ernest was the only one at the Christmas celebration in our church; the service was all in English. Last year we could not attend the divine service for months because it was forbidden to preach in German. This last year it was half in English and half in German. At the next meeting they will vote on what will be done in 1920.

Thanks for all your good wishes. I also wish you happiness, good health, and success in your business. How was business this year? We were glad to hear of good crops in Switzerland. Here the wheat and corn were quite good. It is almost a miracle that the corn was so good because it was very dry in the early summer and fall. My garden dried up very early. Apples were scarce here. There are some shipped in, but they are very expensive. I am glad for your sake that you have a lot of apples. But the epidemic that hit your cattle is terrible. Can the meat be used for human food? We hope for you that the cattle will soon be cured.

Here in our country the terrible flu was as bad as it was with you. The dying was pitiful. We read that no country was spared. Because of this flu, Hans[1] and his group were held back for three weeks and then came the armistice. Oh, we'd better not talk of all the anxiety and sorrow we had to bear in that time. I do want to mention that Hans got married Oct. 19, 1918. On Oct. 22, he was supposed to go to California to a camp and afterwards to Russia. Oh, I believe I could not have survived that. You will say that we were not the only ones, and that is right. Here and in the neighborhood seventy young men went away, and some did not return. They sleep their last sleep in foreign soil. Enough of it. Everyone is longing for true peace! There is such unrest everywhere. Everything one buys is so high and often bad quality, especially

139

material and dresses. It is hard to say where it will go. Let us trust in our highest help.

So you like our grandchild. The stork can come again any hour. The little girl was a year old Dec. 8, and she can already walk. She is big and strong for her age. It would be nice if the next child were a boy.[2]

Willie married Margaretha Hansen Oct. 7. Her parents are also farmers, but they live in town now. Hans's wife's maiden name was Anna Walters. Both couples were with us at Christmas. It is getting quiet here now again. Only the youngest is still at home. He seems to be the tallest of all, Fred is almost as tall, then Hans. Willie is the shortest; Hans the fattest.

Every day I am expecting a letter from our niece Bertha. We wonder if she will come to America. I would be so happy, but I don't want to encourage or discourage anyone, for one never knows how people will react to the conditions here. If Bertha came, it would be much safer if she could join a family. There is also the question of what her father and mother will say to it. If she were only here already, she could stay with us as long as she liked. I suggest she should take some sewing lessons. If she learns English fast, she could take a job in an office.

New Year's Eve.

This has been a bitter cold day with some snow and a strong north wind. I hope there won't be a snow storm. Yesterday was beautiful and warm. We have already had real winter weather with lots of snow which is not gone.

How glad we all were who had the corn picked before the snow came. Our Ernest was fortunate because he had picked his. In many places there is still corn in the fields. Ernest picked sixty acres. It has to be done ear by ear by hand and thrown into the wagon. I don't know if you have seen real corn. It is a beautiful plant. Six hundred – eight hundred – a thousand. They stand in rows close together like soldiers.

I am sending you pictures of my sons, and I hope you will enjoy them, especially dear Mother. I had a Christmas card from Aunt Lina in Columbus. She apologizes for not writing to me and to Switzerland. She will write soon, but she is always very busy. I am glad that Julia is all right; walking on crutches must be hard. Greetings to her, to the cousins, and Bertha.

I have come to an end. I hope that your winter won't be too harsh.
Best wishes and greetings to all.
Write soon!
Louise Ritter

---

[1]Hans was drafted, but he never left home.
[2]The first grandchild was Fred's daughter; she was named Marie Louise after her grandmother.

INTRODUCTORY NOTE
For Letters of June 8, December 6 and 7, 1920

Louise's reaction to news of her mother's death was calm, almost unemotional. She spoke of the "happy reunion which cannot be too far away" and asked, "Did the beloved one speak of me?" Her grief had not been as controlled when Emma, Rudolf, and her father died. She had said of Emma's death "like a thunderbolt the news hit me," and continued, "Oh, God, how heavy rests your hand on us!" The following year Rudolf had died. Her grief never again was as painfully expressed as in those letters when she feared for her sanity. After her father's death she wrote to her mother: "Never again can I look into the eyes of my dear father; maybe not into yours either!" Louise's fears came true; twenty-seven years had passed since she had last seen her mother.

The invitations for those in Switzerland to come to America were repeated, but with little expectation that they would be heeded. She had more hope that Bertha might come. Letters were enjoyed, but she repeated her wish, "It would be still nicer if we could be together and talk to each other." Anna and her family were the only ones left; her parents were dead and her brother rarely wrote. Those in Nebraska had little interest in the content of the letters.

The neighborhood continued to change with old friends and Swiss born friends and acquaintances leaving or dying. In 1920 in the entire state there were only 1,808 foreign born from Switzerland.[1]

The church no longer provided the same refuge for Louise as it had before the war. The members by a two-thirds majority had decided that the services on the first and third Sundays of the month would be in English and all the rest and holidays in German. In May of the same year it was decided to get Evangelical Hymnals for use in English Services.[2]

Once again there was financial insecurity after the high prices of the war years. In the middle of 1920, foreign demand for agricultural products fell sharply, and government price guarantees for wheat expired. The effect was startling. Wheat, which had sold for $2.02 per bushel in December 1, 1919, brought only $1.31 per bushel in December 1, 1920. During the same period corn dropped from $1.22 to $.41, oats from $.65 to $.37. For agriculture and Nebraska, the Twenties were years of depression rather than prosperity in spite of relatively good crops and many superficial signs of prosperity.[3]

These economic facts accounted for Louise's questions concerning her inheritance from her mother. She had not seen any of her family in Switzerland for twenty-seven years. The needs of her sons and their young families were of immediate concern. With these new families she had established a ritual: "Sundays were for the children."

Dear Sister and Family,

Yesterday with deep sorrow we received the sad news of the death of our dear mother and grandmother. How sorry I am that I did not write earlier. Please excuse me, Sister, and I hope and believe that our dear mother would forgive me. Already two months ago I had a four page letter ready to mail, but unfortunately I had no envelope and then my letter was out of date. I should have sent a card to announce the birth of Anna Eleanor Ritter[4] and to wish a quick recovery to Mother, but I wanted to wait for the next happy news. On May 8, Hans and Anna had a little daughter who was baptized in the home on June 6. Her name is Marjorie Clara.[5] Father and I were her godparents. Who would have thought then that our dear mother had already been in her grave for three weeks. The death announcement arrived yesterday. I hope she did not have to suffer much. Did the beloved one speak of me? Now she is released from all earthly sufferings and let us hope united with our dear ones who went before her. The Lord be kind to her, and we hope of a happy reunion which cannot be too far away.

I am happy the pictures came on time so Mother could enjoy them. You were right about the boys, dear Sister; but you are mistaken about my not having gray hair. I have some, not very many, but I am content. It is time for me, and gray hair is nothing to be ashamed about. You would not recognize me; I am heavier now. I have weighed one hundred and sixty pounds since last winter.

How is business? Tell me about it. We had a cold, wet spring. We couldn't sow oats until the end of April and the beginning of May. The corn was still to be planted. We did plant ours by the end of May. We had so much work that we were too tired to write in the evenings, and Sundays belong to the children.

I understand that Alfred[6] is working for a farmer. If he came to America, he could be well paid working for his cousins, working with horses and machinery. I have been waiting for a letter from Bertha since Christmas and for her arrival, but in vain. She intended to come here, but now we don't hear any more from her. If you know anything, do tell me. Good girls find good jobs here and are paid up to $10 a week. I hope you and your family are in good health. Did you have the flu last winter? There was some here in the spring, but fortunately not so bad as last year. Are your cattle well again? We'll hope so.

Please excuse my bad handwriting. I am much disturbed by Mother's death. Also, my right arm is bad. Often in the mornings I can hardly move it. It is as if something is turning in the arm, and I have terrible pain. My whole right side is affected by arthritis, including the right foot where I have three corns and bad callouses.

How are Julia, Uncle Wilhelm, and Aunt Grittli? Please write soon and much about your children. I am serious about Alfred if he wants to come. There are many new and interesting things for him here, and if he should not like it, he could go back. Please think it over. We here are among decent people, and there are no conceited ones Father always says.

How much do potatoes and sugar cost you? Everything is high here, machinery, dresses, and shoes,[7] and it is getting worse.

Best greetings to all
Your Sister and Aunt
Louise Ritter

Tilden, December 6, 1920

Dear Sister and Family,

A few weeks ago I received your letter, just half a week after I mailed mine. They must have met halfway, perhaps in New York.

Recently a report came from Mr. Stucki, an attorney, in regard to our inheritance. I have not yet answered it because we don't quite understand it. I would like to know how things are in Erlach, how our sister-in-law is, and if Brother Fritz has by now cleared up the old affairs. The disclosures seem pretty bad to me. I can't understand why he had let things go so carelessly and had not even paid the interest. Didn't his wife inherit quite a bit? I do hope that all comes to a good end. Has the sister-in-law had her operation and how is she? Please, dear Sister, tell me all about it.

Did Heidi[8] learn a profession and is she perhaps a teacher? How old is Fritz's son? You see how little I know about my brother and his family. Did you inform your son Alfred that he would find well-paid employment here? With us he would not be so much in a foreign land as he is in France,[9] but of course he would be further away from parents and brothers and sisters. But he could return if he did not like it.

The man of whom I wrote, Mr. Gottfred Lerch,[10] is leaving Dec. 7 for Switzerland. He could not get his passport before the beginning of November, so he harvested his corn and last week he auctioned all his belongings. When he returns, he will go straight to Kansas and from there to Oregon where he intends to settle for good. In Kansas at his brother's he will meet his wife and their five children, who will all leave Tilden tomorrow. Henry Koltmann will travel with Lerch, but will return here to his wife and two children. As I mentioned in my previous letter, this would be a good opportunity for Alfred or Bertha in Bern to travel with them, or better still both of them. So think it over carefully. The two men will return to this country in February. I surely hope when Lerch visits you, you will receive him kindly. He deserves it; the whole family is welcome wherever they go. But should he not be able to visit you because of the epidemic, I would be very sorry and

143

would not know what to do. Please let me know, dear Sister, when he can expect one of you. I will surely give Mr. Lerch your address.

Congratulations to the new grandparents and the new grandson and his parents.

Soon Christmas will be here and a new year will begin. The Lord's richest blessings, happiness, and health to you for both holidays. Our dear mother celebrates Christmas now with her dear ones who have gone before her. Now they will never be separated again. Who knows when we may follow them? God alone knows. I often look at your nice family picture. It is a great joy to me, but it would be still nicer if we could be together again and talk to each other. Who knows, perhaps one day we can.

Two weeks ago our corn was all picked. Many have not yet finished picking. At the beginning and at the end of the picking we had some snow, and today it is so dark that we might get more. It is no easy task to pick corn in the snow when the hands and feet get very cold. There is much corn, but the price is low.[11] Everything that the farmer has to sell is cheap, but what he has to buy is very expensive and of poor quality. Sugar is cheaper now after the time of canning is over. Sorry that I cannot send along a box of something for your children, but they say the customs officers are very strict, and I don't want to give Mr. Lerch any trouble. If he could buy a small brass pan for me, I would be very happy. The pan need be smoked only a little.[12]

How are you all? How are the children? I hope all are well just as we are and that you'll stay well through the winter. Oh, how much all your children have grown, especially Alfred and the three girls. I wish you could all come to America! What a celebration that would be!

I hope to hear from you soon. Perhaps the children would not mind writing for you if you are too busy!

Many greetings to you all –
Louise Ritter

Lerch told me that his brother lives in Zielbrucke, not far from you. Perhaps one of your sons can go there and get some information.

Tilden, December 7, 1920

Dear Ones,

This morning I mailed my letter, and tomorrow, Dec. 8, the Swiss-Americans will depart instead of today as I stated. The bringer of these lines is Mr. Gottfred Lerch, for two years our nearest neighbor. I hope you will have some good hours together. Ask whatever you would like to know; he will be glad to tell you all.

Best greetings from all to all – your
L. Ritter

[1]Sheldon, *Nebraska,* I, p. 193.

[2]Minutes of Evangelical Friedens Church, 11 Jan. and 14 May 1920.

[3]Olson, *History of Nebraska,* pp. 295-296.

[4]Second child of her oldest son, Fred.

[5]First child of Hans.

[6]Alfred is Anna's youngest son, twenty years old now. In 1920 unemployment rose to more than 130,000 in Switzerland. This is almost a fifth of the population. World War I devoured the savings accumulated during a century of prosperity by four generations of Swiss. Martin, *Switzerland,* pp. 265-266.

[7]Coats cost $25 to $65; dresses, $5.75 to $16.50; work shoes, $4.50 to $6.00; dress shoes, $7.35 to $7.85. *Tilden Citizen,* 4 June 1920, p. 4.

[8]The oldest child of her brother Fritz, who is the same age as Louise's Ernest.

[9]"At the end of World War I France had severe shortage of manpower. Had it not been for the more than a million and a half foreign workers whom France received in the years from 1920 to 1928 – most of them from Italy, Switzerland, and Belgium – the country would have been less populous at the outbreak of the Second World War in 1939 than it had been when it faced the First World War a generation earlier." Stuart H. Hughes, *Contemporary Europe: A History,* 2nd ed. (Englewood Cliff, New Jersey: Prentice Hall, Inc., 1966), p. 137.

[10]The advertisement in the 19 November 1920, *Tilden Citizen,* p. 8, illustrates the type of equipment on a typical Nebraska farm at the time. Spelling errors were in the sale bill. (See p. 146)

[11]Corn prices had fallen from $1.45 in 1919 to $.41 in December of 1920. Olson, *History of Nebraska,* p. 115.

[12]For customs purpose – so it would pass as a used utensil.

145

PUBLIC SALE

As I have decided to quit farming and move to Oregon, I will sell the following described property at Public Auction to the highest bidder on the farm known as the Arnold Uhlman place, 2 miles due west of Tilden, Nebraska.

DECEMBER 2

Free Lunch at Noon by Osborn   **Sale immediately after**

8   HEAD HORSES   8

1 team black geldings coming 9 years old, weight 2400; 1 bay mare about 14 years old, weight 1300; 1 bay mare about 11 years old, weight 1100; 1 bay mare coming 4 years old, weight 1200.

16   HEAD CATTLE   16

Consisting of six fairly good milch cows, 8 yearlings and 2 spring calves.

About 20 aging shoats and 6 fall pigs.

FARM MACHINERY

Spring wagon, wagon with triple box, old wagon with box, wagon with rack, Milwaukee 7 ft. binder with new canvas, Milwaukee 5 ft. mower, Champion 5 ft mower, McCormick hay rake, Jenkins overshot hay stacker, hay sweep, Independence 6 ft. mower, Janesville lister with drill, 3 cultivators, corn planter, Demster press drill, one row drill, gang plow-14 inch, John Deere plow-16 inch, walking plow-14 inch, disc, three section harrow with cart, bobsled, manure spreader, 3 ideal hog waterers, feed bunk, 3 sets harness.

HOUSEHOLD GOODS

1 Majestic range, neatly new; 1 Round Oak heater, 1 3-burner oil stove, 1 organ, 1 combined bookcase and writing desk, 1 6-foot dining room table, 4 dining room chairs, 2 rockers, 1 dresser, 2 beds, 1 kitchen cabinet, 1 cupboard, 1 Economy King 60 capacity cream separator, some dishes and kitchen untensils, canned fruit, vegetables and general farm tools too numerous to mention. About 10 dozen mixed chickens, 1 stack alfalfa.

Gottfried Lerch, Owner

INTRODUCTORY NOTE
For Letters of June 27 and December 28, 1921
and February 9, 1922

The trip to Switzerland, so long dreamed about, almost materialized. It is difficult to judge whether Louise really looked forward to the trip or if she was a little afraid of the changes she would have found. She was haunted by memories of the unpleasant boat trip across the ocean.[1] Her niece Klara said: "I am sure that your grandmother would not have wanted anymore to live in Switzerland. But it was a pity that she was not allowed to pay at least once more a visit in her old homeland."[2]

Louise had established her own family rituals in Nebraska. In early letters she had been critical of the Christmas trees available. Now she invited all the children for Christmas and boasted: "We had a beautiful tree with candles and decorations just like you." This group included ten adults and four grandchildren.

The following letters include memories of persecutions during the war years, statements of economic concerns, and reports of failing health. Her pain might have been responsible for a note of impatience. She really had hoped for the companionship of Bertha but had been disappointed again; Louise continued, almost out of habit, to offer those in Switzerland good reasons for coming to Nebraska. But even a Swiss tenant failed to live up to expectations.

Tilden, June 27, 1921

Dear Sister,

I received your letter of the 25th and feel guilty. I should have written earlier; please excuse me. Your letter arrived in February, and soon after that I had a bad attack of rheumatism in my right arm and hand which pulled my five fingers together. I had to have my arm in a sling for some time.

How nice it would have been if Bertha had come with Mr. Lerch, but it would have been too good to be true. She had written to me so anxiously, and I told her all in detail. Then she let me wait for a year or more, and finally she didn't come. Well, I'll stay away from inviting anyone to come here. Right now I would get little thanks for it. We have already had a terrific heatwave in June. This noon it was 100 degrees in the shade, and at two o'clock it was even hotter. Then there were dark clouds and it thundered, but they passed on and we did not have a drop of rain. Although it has been only ten days since we had rain, the crops are beginning to suffer.[3] Some places there was hail. My garden is dried up already, and two weeks ago it was so beautiful. There is no fruit on the trees this year. For three weeks we each had a little

147

dish of strawberries at noon and in the evening. I preserved twelve quarts, but the few apples which survived the frost in the spring are wormy and fall off the trees, and we have no cherries. Fortunately, I still have a good supply of preserves from last year. I hope that you have a good crop.

June 20. So Mr. Lerch did not come to you a second time! Sorry. He could have brought me the brass pan. It was not just the pan I wanted; it would have been a nice remembrance of our mother, who surely used a utensil like that very often. I have never seen one here nor in a catalog.

You know what, dear Sister? You could take a trip to come see us. Wouldn't that be nice in the fall? That is the best season here. You did give up your business and can get away easily. Fritz would like to visit you if he could travel with some friends. There is one thing that concerns us and keeps us from making the trip. We would rather travel via Hamburg and Basel than through France. I would like to hear your opinion about it. Is it really unsafe, even dangerous because of the black troops? We read in the papers about many assaults and murders. I have asked a lot of questions at once, haven't I? Oh, if we could only get together once, it would be so much better than writing!

I cannot give away something that I don't have. Dear Sister, you will understand what I mean! No, I didn't get any thanks for it, and I won't write about that matter. I am surprised that you are so helpful. That's all very well, but you have nine children and he only two.[4] Honestly, I cannot understand how he could take that away from Emma's children. Here the prices have not improved since I wrote to you last. They have gone down even more. My sons had to go into debt to carry through, but all think with God's help they will pull through and with hard work.[5]

Please don't be angry with me as you were the other time I gave you my opinion. Just as the other time, I don't mean you. You'd better burn this letter after you have read it.

Dear Sister, would you please ask Attorney Stucki to send me a receipt as to the matter of the inheritance. Many thanks in advance. We can't understand why he has not done that long ago. We have nothing in our hands. I asked him long ago to invest the money for an undetermined time so that we can withdraw it any time. Please answer as soon as possible.

Best greetings to all across the ocean. I hope to see you soon.
Your Sister and the children in our family,
L. Ritter
God's blessing to the young couple. How far is France from you?

Tilden, December 28, 1921

Dear Sister and Family,

I received your letter. I think it took eighteen days to get here. It was

148

impossible to answer it straight away as I had to do a lot for Christmas. We invited all the children for Christmas dinner and for the giving of presents afterwards. We had a beautiful tree with candles and decorations just like you. The presents lay around the tree with the names of the givers and the receivers. They were not only for the children, but also for the grown-ups. Everybody came and received. Fred's mother-in-law was here also. She couldn't help crying since it was the first Christmas without her husband. Fritz Clausen died suddenly on Monday morning, July 18, without having been sick.

We had a lovely time. Too bad you couldn't be with us. I hope your Christmas was happy also. The Yankees don't celebrate New Year's Day. I don't know what we will do on New Year's Day. Much depends on the weather. Last year we were at Hans's.

Our weather seems to have been much like yours. Early summer brought enough rain. The corn crop was good; wheat, mediocre; fruit, a complete failure; vegetables, good. In November we had very cold weather and only a little snow early in December. Then it became very cold, and at Christmas we had a thin cover of snow. Since then it has been mild and sunny. All through the fall we had a drought, hardly any rain.

So you won't come to visit us. Too bad! You are many years younger than we and could travel more easily. Besides, you would come to an entirely strange land and would find many new and interesting things. But it would be wonderful for us to see our old, beloved homeland again.

If our agent in Omaha had not made us wait until Sept. 3, which was too late for us, we would have come to you and perhaps still be there. You didn't know that, did you!

You once asked if I knew English. No, but I can get about fairly well in the shops and so. I had too little opportunity to learn English. One can speak German again without having to fear being beaten. There was a time when it was forbidden to prevent attention and because of the rudeness of fanatics. So we chatted in English as well as we could. The nasty aftereffect of hatred one will feel for a long time.[6]

Business is poor. What one has to buy is high, but prices for what we sell are low. For example, a year ago a bushel of corn was 40¢ and now it is 23¢ to 25¢. In addition, the taxes are high.[7] Complaining doesn't help; let's hope for better times.

This morning a long-time Swiss neighbor died, Mrs. Emmanuel Bossard.[8] You seem to celebrate a wedding every few months. You will soon be all alone. Good luck to you all and also to my niece Anna who is expecting a baby. I can well understand how you love your grandchild; we too love ours. They all run around so happily.

The day before yesterday I had a telegram from Attorney Stucki asking if he should send me the interest. I was so frightened until I read it. Of course the agent couldn't read it and phoned us. The attorney had never written before. Fritz always wonders why the bank over there does not send a report of our holdings. If we stay well, we may come over in the spring. Fritz says it is all right. I cannot say for myself. If I get worse, I must go to a doctor and I hate that. Oh, if only Bertha Konig had come back with Lerch! I would have some one with me and could rest a bit more. Don't worry about me; I can get along.

It is nice that Julia visits you once in a while. I often think of her. Where does she live now? How is her health? If you could only give as a present the mentioned interest! But this would involve so much writing and that makes me so tired. Greetings to her as well as to Konigs in Iffwyl and Elise Schurch and Marie Berger.

To all of you dear relatives, best greetings and wishes for a blessed New Year.

It often seems too hard that our dear mother is no longer with us.

Our sons and also Father are well and very busy. I hope that winter won't be too harsh after New Year's Day.

Write soon.

Your

L. Ritter

Tilden, February 9, 1922

Dear Sister and Family,

A few days ago we received a letter from Attorney Stucki in regard to our dear mother's inheritance. We had not understood the telegram correctly as Mr. Stucki guessed. I can't understand now how it could have happened. We thought the telegram referred to the interest, but it was inquiring if we wished Mr. Stucki to send us the whole legacy plus interest. We could have inquired here at the bank about the exchange rate of the currency, but as it is, there was a lot of unnecessary correspondence because of the mis-understanding. My apologies. I immediately instructed Mr. Stucki to send us the legacy now if the currency exchange was still the same. We can make good use of it and can help our sons in these hard times.

How are all of you? I hope you are all well. How are your daughter Anna and your two children in France?[9] Are they safe there, or is it true that France expels Swiss[10] people? Newspaper reports are often false, and I hope they are in this case. How are the others?

So far winter has not been bad, and if it doesn't get worse we should be content. We have had snow now for almost two weeks. It stayed on after the last storm on Febr. 1 since it had rained hard the evening before. The sidewalks are icy and many broke their arms. I hope that you also have not had too bad a winter. If Ernst gets together with Mr. Stucki, the two men could discuss matters more. Father tells me Mr. Stucki should send 10,000 fr.[11] and leave the rest at the bank with interest if the currency is still the same. If our trip to Switzerland this summer should materialize, the other matter could be straightened out then. Otherwise we will have to do it by correspondence.

I hope, dear Sister, that you and yours are well and that you now have two grandchildren. We enjoy our four grandchildren so much.[12] Louise can say almost everything now, naturally in English. The others also are beginning to chatter. It won't be long and all four will be able to speak better English than we grandparents.

I am feeling better now. There is a lot of work to do. We butchered this week, and yesterday I rendered down thirteen gallons of lard. Today I made a cheese. I now have six already and will continue making them until I am tired or have no rennet anymore. It is only 10¢ a pound. We have not yet received a penny for our leased farm this year. It is the first time in all these years that we have had such a tenant. Business is bad, but that fellow has no will power. And he is a Swiss!

I will close now. Please give Mr. Stucki the information. I thank you for all the trouble you are taking on my behalf. Best greetings,
Your,
Louise Ritter and Family

[1]Personal knowledge. Often related by Fritz Ritter.

[2]Information in a letter to the author from Klara Stucki of Ins, Switzerland, 4 April 1978.

[3]The years 1921 to 1940 are recorded as a dry period with only one wet year – 1923. Olson, *History of Nebraska*, p. 13.

[4]Evidently, as is the situation so often in families, there was a disagreement on the settlement of the inheritance. This refers to her father's estate.

[5]There was a financial depression in the country in 1921. "Nebraska in 1920 was sailing on the highest tide of prosperity the state had ever known.... The sudden notice from the federal reserve centers that bank credit must be curtailed was, in fact, a notice to millions of farmers and stockmen to sell their stuff and reduce their notes at their banks.... In 1921 prices of live stock and grain on Nebraska farms and ranches fell from 30 percent to 40 percent. Thousands of farmers who had bought live stock on borrowed money, found themselves, after selling their live stock at forced sale, still in debt at their banks and the means of paying the debt diminishing from day to day." Sheldon, *Nebraska* I, pp. 983-984.

[6]Because of the difficulties they had during World War I, the Evangelical Friedens Church did not print church notices in the local paper again until 1923.

For further comments see the Introductory Notes for 1916 through 1918.

[7]Including corn, wheat, oats, barley, potatoes, cattle, and hogs and all other products, "the average farm price index in Nebraska from 1922 to 1925 was slightly less than thirty-five percent above prewar level. During the same time, however, the wholesale price index averaged slightly more than forty-four percent above the prewar level. Another factor affecting the farmer's economic position – and even more, his outlook – was the high tax schedule. Most farm taxes were paid in the form of the general property tax, and at no time in the Twenties did levies fall below 122 percent of the 1913 levy.... Expressed another way, taxes which took 5.63 per-

cent of average farm net income in 1914 absorbed 20.41 percent in 1922, 13.48 percent in 1924 . . . .", Olson, p. 297.

[8]Mrs. Bossard was a neighbor who was Louise's age. She and her husband had come from Switzerland. They, too, always spoke the Swiss-German and were early and faithful members of the Evangelical Friedens Church. Her death left Louise more alone.

[9]After World War I there was a brief period of prosperity and then high unemployment in Switzerland. Many went to France to work. Martin, *Switzerland,* p. 265.

[10]Part of the difficulty with France concerned free tariff zones. Martin, p. 268.

[11]At an exchange rate of five francs to the dollar, it would be about $2,000.

[12]Harold Ritter, the first child of Willie, is the fourth grandchild.

INTRODUCTORY NOTE
For Letters of January 1923

Louise wrote: "We did not give up our trip, but one thing after the other happened." It was now easier to think about the trip than to actually take it. She even failed to ask her Swiss relatives when they were coming to Nebraska. Instead of making the trip, Louise and Fritz retired. She was now sixty, and he was sixty-four. She moved into another new house Fritz built for her. This one was smaller and in town. She would have less work.

Living across from the church had benefits. She could attend special functions now. Fritz became more involved in church work. In January, he was one of three members of a building committee to study the feasibility of constructing a basement under the church. He was also chosen as a delegate to the District Conference in Falls City, Nebraska.[1] For the first time since the war, weekly church notices were placed in the local paper: "First and third Sunday in the month, services in the American language; second, fourth and fifth Sunday in the month services in the German language."[2]

In this letter, as so often before, Louise wrote of the cycle of the seasons and the cycle of birth and death. Her final page reported the construction of the highway for cars being built where nearly thirty years ago they had seen Indians on horseback and where they had traveled so often in horse and buggy. This highway and their retirement to town completed another cycle.

Tilden, January 1923

Dear Sister and Family,

I received your letter on Dec. 27, and the previous one in the spring. I meant to write, but did not get to it. We did not give up our trip, but one thing after the other happened. First, we had a lot of cherries, and they had to be canned. I have over one hundred quarts in the cellar. Second, Fritz had bought a building site in town last spring and had a nice, friendly house built last summer so that we can retire there. The interior is not quite finished; it still needs some painting and the bathroom is not complete. We did not hurry with it since we can still live here. But it is time to retire; we are getting old. Fritz is better than I. When rheumatism plagues me, I cannot write; and lately my hands and feet hurt me badly. The last few days I felt a bit better.

On New Year's Day it started to snow, but it is not too cold. It was cold in Oct. and Nov., but Dec. was mild and dry.

We had much rain at the end of July and the beginning of August. This spoiled the grain harvest somewhat, but it did a lot more good for our corn.

Then it was dry again. We had many apples and potatoes; not so much hay, etc. We have to thank God that He supplies us so well with all that is necessary and that He gives us health. Dear Aunt was called away so quickly; I wish her rest and heavenly peace. I was very surprised to receive a legacy from her. You were the first one who wrote to me about it. Something must have been lost. I wish Aunt Grittli had received it. After we find out about it, I would like to pass it on to her.

In April, Hans's father-in-law died from a stroke. His wife now feels very lonely. At Christmas we all were at Hans's; on New Year's Day they all were here. We had happy festive days. Last summer Willie built a new house. We all wish his wife Margaretha better health. Her boy is so strong, and his mother has to suffer so long from the flu – it is so sad. The other children are all well. Strahms have two grown-up daughters, also Fritz Oppliger.[3]

I am glad you are all well and also the children in France. Your family continues to grow and instead of little children, you have big ones now and little grandchildren and a daughter-in-law. Best wishes to the newly engaged couple. God's blessing on their way! Aren't any of Emma's daughters married or Heidi in Erlach?

Last summer, some highways were constructed here in Nebraska. One passes our farm. It was so interesting to watch those people. There was a group of Negroes among them. When they approached, there was a lot of traffic on the road as if the military had moved in. The largest machine or grader was drawn by sixteen mules, and what dust it stirred in that dry weather – it was horrible. Now we have a fine road which will be used much next summer by cars from near and far.[4] Already last summer the traffic was very heavy here. Since almost every bridge is torn out and new ones being built, the traffic is directed north or south until everything is fixed. Therefore we don't have much traffic here at present. For almost four weeks we had campers on our place who worked on the road and built cement culverts. They were the foreman and his wife, who cooks for them and five workmen, nice young people. They lived in a large tent and wagon. Now all is in order again, and today is Jan. 8, and the north wind has been blowing all day, but it is not cold. The snow is gone, but there may be new snow – winter is far from over yet.

Happy New Year and God's blessing. Don't be cross that I write so seldom – write soon.

Louise Ritter

[1]Minutes of the Evangelical Friedens Church, 28 January 1923.

[2]*Tilden Citizen*, 5 January 1923, p. 1.

[3]Mrs. Strahm is their niece, daughter of Rosetti. Fritz Oppliger and his wife immigrated from Switzerland to Tilden in 1909.

[4]Highway 275 was being built. Its route has been changed since then.

INTRODUCTORY NOTE
For Letter of December 16, 1923

Louise's sons have become prosperous farmers in the area. In the *Tilden Citizen* on March 23, 1923, William Ritter is reported having shipped one car of hogs; Hans, one car of cattle; and on April 6 Ernest shipped five cars of hogs. May 8 of the same year Fred Ritter, Jr. is reported sending two cars of cattle. She had this family about her and could enjoy their successes.

The distance between herself and her Swiss family increased. If there was a misunderstanding, it took too long to clarify the problem. Nothing could stop her concern for the family members even though she had never seen most of the children she worried about.

In a sense Louise was a stranger everywhere. She was not of Nebraska nor was she any longer a part of Switzerland.

Tilden, December 16, 1923

Dear Sister and Family,

Please excuse my writing with pencil; I hope you can decipher it.

Since March 27 we have lived in town, just across from the Evangelical Church, our church. I told you last winter about our move. But I never heard from you and I wonder why. Perhaps I again did something wrong, or whatever may be the case. But all the same I want to send you all the best for the new year. May it be a good one for you. While my note travels across the sea, we here and you there are celebrating a Merry Christmas. How are your children in France? I often am worried about those two. In Germany the misery must be great.[1] May God be merciful and change unhappiness to blessings.

I hope you, dear Sister, and all are in good health.

Last summer I had visitors from Columbus, Ohio. Aunt Lina Kunz and her daughter Anna with her eleven year old foster son Henri came and stayed ten days.

Once more, congratulations and best greetings to all –
Louise Ritter

---

[1] In Germany organized groups of veterans committed acts of terrorism. Both Communists and extreme nationalists made many attempts in the immediate postwar years to take over the various state governments as well as the central government in Berlin. There was disastrous inflation in Germany. By the end of 1923 the value of the mark sank to almost nothing. The result was that all who owed money were able to pay off their debts in worthless currency, and all who were owed money found their assets wiped out. Easton, *The Western Heritage*, pp. 749-750.

Olga Johnson Ritter

Ernest Ritter

156

INTRODUCTORY NOTE
For letter of August 1924

William S. Bernard in his book *Americanization Studies* presents a list of what he identifies as the immigrants' wishes. The first is the desire for new experience, which includes change, danger, instability, and social irresponsibility. The second is the desire for security, which resulted in caution and conservatism. This desire led immigrants to incorporate within an organization – family, community, church, or state. The third is the craving for the appreciation of others. The final desire is for recognition, which includes securing distinction in the eyes of the public.[1]

The "desire for new experiences" has little relationship to Louise and Fritz, but the other desires can be substantiated by Louise's letters and the recorded experiences of her family. The last desire, recognition, came slowly. The war years had made Fritz and Louise again feel like outsiders in the community. Reports on Fritz and his sons shipping livestock to Omaha and Chicago appeared in the local paper, an acknowledgeent of the family's financial success. Their names appeared in accounts of church activities but not in the social columns. The local paper included no mention of their new home or their move to Tilden.

The first social comment came with the report of the marriage of their youngest son. "The groom is a son of Mr. and Mrs. Fritz Ritter and is a young man of sterling repute in this community where he has grown to manhood."[2] In her letters, Louise expressed no desire to be a part of the social activities; she was too busy with her work. She often did admit to loneliness.

For years the letters she received had been a major social event in her life. Because of this, one is pleased to find in the August 1924 letter a return to the tone of earlier letters. Louise again asked her relatives to visit. Maybe the letter from Fritz Marti, a reminder of their childhood in Switzerland, helped to inspire her. She tried to keep her Nebraska family interested and would read the letters to "those who would listen," but she found a more interested audience among immigrant neighbors. She would share with them the news of their common homeland.[3] There were not many of them still living who could understand and share her "divided heart."

While Louise's sons had little interest in the letters from Switzerland, they remained loyal in their love for and duty toward their parents. Hans and Fred could barely remember their journey, and Willie and Ernest had no memories to draw from. Louise and Fritz were spared the experience of many immigrants who were rejected by their children. The immigrant parents hoped for a better life for their children. Ironically, the second generation often felt it necessary to be fully accepted by the American society to be successful; and to accomplish this, they often moved away from or rejected their parents, who were denied such acceptance.[4] Sometimes

157

there were violent quarrels which resulted in separation, while other times the children drifted away in the tradition of American mobility. Closer family ties in the Old World tradition tended to survive in rural communities where there was a concentration of one nationality.[5] Louise's children had not lived in a Swiss settlement, but they had grown up in a rural community with many Swiss and German immigrants.

After their retirement, it was difficult for both Louise and Fritz to accept the change in their roles, but she could write: "The golden youth belongs to our children. One helps as much as one can." Work had been a major part of their lives too long for them to easily accept idleness. Both their Swiss heritage and Reformed creed had taught that labor was not merely for economic reasons but also for a spiritual end. The pursuit of economic success called for the virtues of diligence and thrift.[6]

Tilden, End of August, 1924

Dear Sister and Family,

At last something from America, I hear you say in my mind. I thought I couldn't write anymore, but I started to try, and I hope you can decipher it with some patience. Imagine, Sister, I received a letter from one of your schoolmates Fritz Marti, formerly a letter carrier in Mulchi. He left Switzerland in 1886 with an uncle who came for a visit and now is in the state of Ohio and has a family and a farm. Perhaps he visited you last year when he was back.

How are you all? Have you had a good year so far? Did you take a trip, and why not to here? Many questions all at once, aren't they? So far we have had a summer as never before. We have to be grateful to the Lord. In the spring it was so dry that we thought there wouldn't be any crop at all. I remember a woman who said to me in June, "Now it is the seventeenth, and every day we will have rain or rather downpours with severe electrical storms." We often have had two in one night and one or two during the day. One night one could have thought the end of the world was near. There were three thunderstorms from nine o'clock on until five in the morning. Many trees were uprooted and broken. There were many lightning flashes, but fortunately no fires or loss of lives. No one could imagine that there would be any corn harvest. We still are not sure of a crop. The corn has grown high, but it is late and well behind its growth in other years. A good hot fall could help a lot – we are hoping for the best. The vegetables are good, and there is plenty of fruit.

It usually gets better than one thinks it will. Our people will finish threshing tomorrow if it doesn't rain overnight.[7] Wheat and oats are fine. Willie threshed at the end of July, and on August 2 he went with his wife and son for a trip to Montana by way of Colorado and Wyoming. He will return soon.

158

Ernest married Miss Olga Johnson on June 1, 1923. She is the daughter of Norwegian immigrants. Her father and mother have been dead for ten years. So we made room for the young couple and moved into town. You, dear Sister, will understand that all work is harder now. The golden youth belongs to our children. One helps as much as one can. Father helped one and then the other during the summer. I am not much good anymore. When I began this letter towards the end of August, I had to stop because I became ill. For weeks I felt miserable and shaky – the letter should have been written long ago. All summer something was wrong with me. Your fine, long letter should have been answered long ago, and I have to beg your pardon. I hope you won't pay me back. How are all of your children? I hope well and happy. Is Martha married? My best wishes to her and Hans. May the Lord bless them and keep them.

A few more years and you will be alone again as we are. This is life, but it hurts that one cannot help anymore. Well, time the comforter of all woes flies quickly by, and soon one has reached one's goal.

Today is fall solstice, and we fear these three weeks. September seldom has a warm day, but also no hard frost. Every sunny day will help the corn as long as it does not freeze. Otherwise, the corn will be soft and cannot be sold and has to be fed to the cattle.

September 30. Yesterday was Hans's birthday.[8] Last Sunday we celebrated our yearly Mission Festival at church. Our house is opposite the church on the north side.

When there is some festivity, everyone brings some food. This is eaten in the church basement, which was dug and bricked only last summer. Before, we went into the country to a shady spot and there we had a church service or another meeting.[9] Do you do something like this now, too?

I must tell you, dear Sister, that Brother Fritz in Erlach never thanked me – he should be ashamed of himself. As if he doesn't know any better. You'd better not say anything; it would only make bad blood.

Don't worry about me; I feel better now. I hope you and the children are all as well as we.
Best greetings to all,
Fred and Louise Ritter and all Children
Write soon again, only I hope that our letters don't cross again like last time. Once again many greetings,
Louise

[1]Bernard, pp. 27-28.
[2]*Tilden Citizen*, 8 June 1923, p. 1.
[3]Interview, Ernest Ritter, January 1979.
[4]Skårdal, *The Divided Heart*, p. 321.

[5]Ibid., pp. 323-324.

[6]Tawney, "Foreword," *The Protestant Ethic and the Spirit of Capitalism,* pp. 2-3.

[7]The brothers and their father had owned their own threshing machine since 1919 or 1920 and worked together harvesting their grain.

[8]Hans was thirty-three years old. He had been four years old when they left Switzerland.

[9]The following item illustrates the church activity to which she referred:

"EVANGELICAL FRIEDENS CHURCH SOCIAL

Last Thursday evening the Ladies Aid met at the home of Mrs. Carolina Michaelson for its monthly meeting out on the beautiful lawn under the most favorable weather conditions. This monthly meeting differed somewhat from the usual gatherings as a special social element was connected with it. The members of the society had invited their husbands and friends and neighbors. Between six and seven supper was served out on the lawn where a large table, which accommodated fifty persons at one time had been erected. About 150 were present. After supper the grab-box feature was pulled out, which afforded considerable amusement and netted a large sum for the Ladies Aid fund. The men were anxious to grab special packages that had been made for them. Ten gallons of ice cream donated by these different parties was served at 10¢ a dish with cake. The evening was spent in playing games, in which the young and old participated. At a late hour everybody departed for their homes, delighted to have had such a splendid time and hoping that we may have such a meeting at least once a year. The ladies were pleased because of the success they met with, as it was the first meeting of such a nature." *Tilden Citizen,* 9 July 1920, p. 1.

This was one of the first references in the paper to this church since the war.

INTRODUCTORY NOTE
For Letter of January 13, 1925

The last letter in this collection begins with Louise's continuing eagerness to share her life with the family in Switzerland. Her family in Tilden was now much larger – four sons and their wives and five grandchildren with two more expected during the new year. The holidays were filled with activities including the three generations of the family. Christmas was celebrated in their home, and they were invited for New Year festivities to their sons. They were a close family unit.

The family did disagree on the language. Louise had insisted that each of her sons learn to write German and speak the Swiss-German. She saw the language of the homeland as symbolic of and essential to their basic patterns of behavior. Swiss-German is not a dialect in the same sense of so many European languages; it is spoken by all Swiss-Germans regardless of education. Once the sons married outside the Swiss group, the loss of the language was inevitable.

Literature reflects this problem as it was confronted by several fictional characters. Beret in *Peder Victorious* is angered by the school's interference in the use of the Norwegian language. Peder was pulled both ways – at home Norwegian was used and in the school it was scorned. Cather in *O Pioneers!* describes the family about the table. "The conversation was all in English. Oscar's wife, from the malaria district of Missouri, was ashamed of marrying a foreigner, and her boys did not understand a word of Swedish." Cather continues by telling that the other brother and his wife did speak Swedish at home but were afraid of being "caught".[1]

Sophus Winther in *Mortgage Your Heart* describes a painful rejection experienced by Meta and Peter. Their son does not want them to come to see him perform in a play. The father understood and said, "I don't think we can mingle very well with Americans. Do you think so, Meta?" He continues, "That's how it is over here in this country, ... we don't really belong when it comes to such things."[2]

The second generation of young people who were struggling to become Americanized could not understand what the language meant to their parents. Winther described its significance: "And so the talk went everywhere plunging at random into the past – the land that was forever young, because it was the home of their childhood and their youth."[3] Louise knew that the loss of the language also indicated the ways of her beloved homeland would be irreparably lost.

Louise's health had been poor for several years. She was not afraid of death. Her unquestioning belief in God and a hereafter where one would be relieved of suffering and pain was a comfort to her. She had suffered mental

161

and physical pain for years. She wrote to her sister: "But you, dear Sister, must not worry – it goes as it goes. We know that everything happens according to God's will. We will trust in Him; He will do it well."

She was to die at home on December 26, 1925, just one day before the birthday of Rudolf. Her funeral services were conducted in her home and in the church across the street.

Louise Ritter cannot be presented as representative of any of the famous Plains literature women such as Beret Holm, Meta Grimsen, Antonia Shimerda, Alexandra Bergson, or Mari Sandoz. She was one of the thousands whose individual stories tell the history of the settlement of the Plains. Her letters reveal the experiences of one individual woman and parallel many of the fictional experiences of heroines of literature. Perhaps it is reasonable to say of her as Cather and Jim Burden say of Antonia, "She was a rich mine of life, like the founder of early races."[4]

Tilden, January 13, 1925

Dear Sister and Family,

Now again the holidays are over and quietness has returned. Dearest Sister, we received your two letters, the second one before Christmas, and I enjoyed them so much. Many thanks also for your good wishes. We also wish you good health and all the best for the new year.

Did your expected visitors come on Christmas Day? I am so sorry I couldn't be with you all for a little while! But we had all our children and grandchildren here on Christmas Eve, except Hans who could not start his car.

Did I tell you that our house is opposite the church? All the children went there first and then came to us where we exchanged gifts and afterwards had coffee and cocoa and cake.

We had real Christmas weather with snow and severe cold. We had a beautiful fall. It was warm up to the first Wednesday in December. We then had snow several times, and the cold was grim – down to 20 degrees below zero. Christmas and New Year's Day were also very cold, and there is no change in sight. Father and I were invited to Fred's on Christmas and to Hans's on New Year's Day. Also the brothers were invited with their families on each day.

Our car is now in winter quarters; and when the sons want us, they get us and take us home again. Tomorrow evening Ernest wants to get us to listen to a great radio concert. Do you also have a radio? Ernest has a loud speaker; Fred also. Here in town there are many. When we lived in the country, we had a radio with ear phones. I heard many a good concert then, but now it is more comfortable.[5] You know, you could give a radio concert once, you with good voices – that would be a marvelous joy to us.

162

So up to now you have six grandchildren. Who knows what the new year will bring us. Frederick, the youngest, is such a darling. He will be two on Febr. 24. Louise and Eleanor recited their verses for the first time in church and did very well. Harold, Willie's little boy, is very shy. None of our grandchildren know any German and won't ever learn it. In the beginning when we found that out, there were many harsh words said. If any of the mothers were of Swiss origin, they would have spoken in the Bern dialect. But now they speak only English. You know, our boys didn't want to speak High German, and their wives don't know Swiss-German. Margaretha doesn't know High, only Low German, and Olga only speaks English.

Do you see, dear Sister, how it is with me? My hands tremble; it is a pity. Since late fall I have been a bit better. In the summer and fall I suffered from dizziness, and that was bad. I do not have to work hard, but I knit and crochet quite a bit.[6] That may not be good for me. But you, dear Sister, must not worry – it goes as it goes. We know that everything happens according to God's will. We will trust in Him; He will do it well.

Father is well, but time is long for him in the winter when he cannot go out. Also, our sons and their families are well. Fred's Eleanor had put her little hand in the fruit press last fall and pinched two fingers so badly that the doctor wanted to amputate them. But after two weeks it was decided it would not be necessary. The previous fall she was so badly hurt by boiling water that her life was in danger. From her behind to her feet large pieces of skin and flesh came off. It was a terrible sight. Poor child has already suffered so much. We all hope that she will have better luck in the future. She always hugs and kisses me when she comes.

I have to close now. I hope you all are well.

Best greetings,

Fritz and Louise Ritter and Children

[1] Cather, *O Pioneers!*, p. 99.

[2] Sophus Keith Winther, *Mortgage Your Heart* (New York: The Macmillan Co., 1937), p. 173.

[3] Ibid., p. 332.

[4] Cather, *My Antonia*, p. 353.

[5] It is never brought out in the letters, but Louise loved music. She played a zither Fritz gave her and often sang with it. Her sons and Fritz often mentioned her love of music and the zither.

[6] "Handiwork by immigrants survived in Old Country patterns during the lifetime of the first generation, seldom beyond. Pioneer housewives were often depicted knitting thick mittens and socks for the whole family, and sewing their clothing from store-bought materials." Skårdal, *The Divided Heart*, p. 251. Louise illustrated this generalization.

Anna and her husband Ernst. She faithfully wrote to Louise from 1893 to 1925.

AFTERWORD

Tilden, Nebraska, December 26th, 1925

Dear Aunt Anna,

It is with regret and sorrow that I must announce to you the death of my mother and your sister, Mrs. Marie Louise Ritter.

She passed to her reward 9:40 this morning after an illness of two weeks at her home.

Funeral Services Tuesday afternoon, Dec. 29th, 1925.

Your nephew,

Fred Ritter Jr.

From Father, Fred, Hans, Willie and Ernest and Families.

This letter concluded the thirty-two years of correspondence between the two families. The next letter from Tilden was sent in 1955. Ernest's daughter asked Fred to tell the family in Switzerland that she hoped to visit them in Bern, Iffwyl, and Ins, as a part of her trip to Europe. This trip resulted in a renewal of communication between the families. Ernest made two trips to Switzerland and met fourteen first cousins. Three of Anna's children – Fritz, Martha, and Klara – came to Tilden. Grandchildren and great-grandchildren of Anna and Fritz have been to Tilden, and great-grandchildren of Louise have visited those in Switzerland. One wishes Louise could have seen this happen.

OBITUARY
DEATH ANGEL CALLS MRS. FRED RITTER SR.

After several weeks spent in a bed of suffering the Death Angel came to relieve Mrs. Fred Ritter Sr. who passed on to her eternal resting place at 9:40 o'clock Saturday morning. Mrs. Ritter was taken seriously ill along about the first of December and was confined to her bed from that time until the end. Previous to this she had been in frail health for a number of years but able to attend to her household duties.

Funeral services conducted by her pastor, Rev. Heckman, were held at the family home at 2 o'clock Tuesday afternoon, followed by services at the Friedens Evangelical Church. Services were given in both German and English. Interment was made in the Odd Fellows cemetery. There was a large attendance of sorrowing relatives and friends.

Marie Louise Siegenthaler was born in Mulchi, Canton Bern, Switzerland, May 3, 1863, and passed from this life December 26, 1925, aged 62 years, 7 months and 23 days. On July 24, 1886, she was united in marriage to Fred Ritter. In the latter part of March 1893, she embarked with her family for America, where they located on a farm in Antelope county, 3½ miles west of Tilden. In 1912 they removed to a smaller farm 1½ miles west of the town where they resided until their retirement from the farm in the spring of 1923. Mr. and Mrs. Ritter together planned a comfortable modern bungalow home in which to enjoy their declining years but in which she was permitted to live only a short time.

She leaves to mourn her death, the sorrowing husband, four sons, Fred Jr., Hans, William and Ernest, all of Tilden, a sister, Mrs. Anna Wuthrich and a brother, Fritz Siegenthaler, both of Canton, Bern, Switzerland. Two sons preceded her in death, one in infancy and Rudolph at the age of ten years. She also leaves seven grandchildren and a host of friends to mourn.

Mrs. Ritter was a woman of ideal character who made and held friends – to know her was to love her. No matter whether in her home or outside she was always the same. The greatest heritage to her loved ones will be the memory of a life well lived.[1]

---

[1]Obituary as it appeared in the *Tilden Citizen*, 31 December 1925, p. 1. Note that Fritz has become Fred, and Rudolf is Rudolph. Louise's husband, Fritz or Fred, died December 30, 1949.

APPENDIX I

Louise's Family

Adele Kunz – Christian Siegenthaler

Marie Louise	b. May 3, 1863	d. December 26, 1925
	(See Appendix III for family)	
Emma	b. 1865	d. 1902
Anna	b. 1869	d. 1952
Fritz	b. 1872	d. 1950

Emma Siegenthaler – Fritz Konig

Anna	b. 1897
Emma	b. 1898
Bertha	b. 1899
Fritz	b. 1902

Anna Siegenthaler – Ernst Wuthrich

Ernst	b. 1893
Fritz	b. 1894
Walter	b. 1895
Otto	b. 1896
Anna	b. 1897
Alfred	b. 1900
Martha	b. 1901
Emma	b. 1905
Klara	b. 1908

Fritz Siegenthaler – Ida

Heidi	b. 1901
Max	b. ?

APPENDIX II
Fritz's Family

Anna Stalder – Johann Ritter
Anna	b. ?	d. ?
Elisabeth	b. 1848	d. 1908
Marianne	b. 1849	d. 1931
Jakob	b. 1850	d. 1951
Fritz (Fred)	b. June 10, 1859	d. December 30, 1949

(See Appendix III for his family)

Rosetta	b. 1863	d. 1943
Elise	b. 1865	d. 1946

Anna – Rudolph Schupbach ?
Rosa (Oppliger)
Hans
Ernst
Rudolph
Marie
Fritz
Anna
Elise

Elisabeth Ritter

Marianne – Uli Whitwer   d. 3 June 1904
Elise
Rosetta

Jakob Ritter

Rosetta – ? Kunz

Lena – Gottfried Strahm

Elise – Gottfried Friedli   d. 25 August 1907

APPENDIX III
Louise Siegenthaler – Fritz Ritter
m. July 24, 1886

Fred   b. April 20, 1887   d. January 25, 1975
                          m. Ella Clausen
   Marie Louise
   Eleanor
   Frederick

Hans   b. September 29, 1888   d. March 30, 1956
                          m. Anna Walters
   Marjorie
(After Louise's death, Delores, Aubyn, Audrey were born)

Rudolf   b. December 27, 1892   d. April 15, 1903

Willie   b. March 10, 1894   d. July 14, 1969
                          m. Margaretha Hansen
   Harold
   Rolland

Ernest   b. July 16, 1901
                          m. Olga Johnson
   Darlene
(After Louise's death, Lois was born)

BIBLIOGRAPHY
Books

Ahlstrom, Sydney E. *A Religious History of the American People*. New Haven: University Press, 1972.

Allen, Durward L. *The Life of Prairies and Plains*. New York: McGraw-Hill Book Co., 1967.

Athearn, Robert G. *Union Pacific Country*. Chicago: Rand McNally and Co., 1971.

Bernard, William S. *Americanization Studies*. Montclair, New Jersey: Patterson Smith, 1971.

Bernard, William S., Carolyn Zeleny, and Henry Miller, eds. *American Immigration Policy*. New York: Harper and Brothers, 1950.

Blegen, Theodore C. *Grass Roots History*. Minneapolis: University of Minnesota Press, 1947.

Blegen, Theodore C., ed. *Land of Their Choice*. St. Paul, Minnesota: University of Minnesota Press, 1955.

Brown, Dee. *The Gentle Tamers*. Lincoln, Nebraska: University of Nebraska Press, 1958

Casey, Robert J. and W.A.S. Douglas. *Pioneer Railroad*. New York: McGraw-Hill Book Co., 1948.

Brunner, Edmund DeS. *Immigrant Farmers and Their Children*. Garden City, New York: Doubleday, Doran, and Co., Inc., 1929.

Cather, Willa. *My Antonia*. Boston: Houghton Mifflin Co., 1961.

----------. *O Pioneers!* Boston: Houghton Mifflin Co., 1962.

Chrisman, Berna Hunter. *When You and I Were Young Nebraska*. Broken Bow, Nebraska: Purcell's Inc. 1971.

Commager, Henry Steele, ed. *Immigration and American History*. Minneapolis: University of Minnesota Press, 1961.

Dawes, Charles G. *A Journal of the McKinley Years*. Ed. Bascom N. Timmons. Chicago: Lakeside Press, 1950.

Dick, Everett. *Conquering the Great American Desert*. Nebraska Historical Society, 1975.

Divine, Robert A. *American Immigration Policy, 1924-1952*. New Haven: Yale University Press, 1957.

Easton, Stewart C. *The Western Heritage*, 2nd ed. New York: Holt, Rinehart, and Winston, Inc., 1966.

Evangelical Catechism. St. Louis: Eden Publishing House, 1929.

Fite, Gilbert C. *American Agriculture and Farm Policy Since 1900.* New York: Macmillan Co., 1964.

----------. *The Farmers' Frontier 1865-1900.* New York: Holt, Rinehart, and Winston, 1966.

Hall, Walter Phelps. *World Wars and Revolution.* New York: D. Appleton-Century Co., 1943.

Handlin, Oscar. *The Uprooted.* Boston: Little, Brown, and Co., 1951.

Hansen, Esther Kolterman. *Along Pioneer Trails in Pierce County, Nebraska,* 1940.

Hansen, Marcus Lee. *The Immigrant in American History.* Cambridge, Massachusetts: Harvard University Press, 1948.

Heaton, Herbert. *Economic History of Europe.* Rev. Ed. New York: Harper & Row, Pub., 1948.

Herold, J. Christopher. *The Swiss Without Halos.* New York: Columbia University Press, 1948.

Hirschfeld, Charles, "The Transformation of American Life." *World War I: A Turning Point in Modern History.* Ed. Jack J. Roth. New York: Alfred A. Knopf, 1968.

History of Antelope County. Henderson, Nebraska: Service Press, Inc., 1976.

Hughes, H. Stuart. *Contemporary Europe: A History,* 2nd ed. Englewood Cliffs, New Jersey: Prentice-Hall, Inc., 1966.

Jones, Maldwyn Allen. *American Immigration.* Chicago: University of Chicago Press, 1960.

Kagan, Donald, et al. *The Western Heritage Since 1648.* New York: Macmillan Co., Inc., 1979.

Kain, Ronald Stuart. *Europe: Versailles to Warsaw.* New York: H.W. Wilson Co., 1939.

Kübler-Ross, Elisabeth, M.D. *Death the Final Stage of Growth.* Englewood Cliffs, New Jersey: Prentice-Hall, Inc., 1975.

----------. *On Death and Dying.* New York: Macmillan Co., 1969.

----------. *Questions and Answers on Death and Dying.* New York: Macmillan Co., 1974.

Kubly, Herbert. *Switzerland.* New York: Time, Inc., 1964.

Lawson, Merlin C., Kenneth F. Dewey, and Ralph E. Neild. *Climatic Atlas of Nebraska.* Lincoln, Nebraska: University of Nebraska Press, 1977.

Leach, A.J. *A History of Antelope County, Nebraska (1868-1883).* Chicago: Lakeside Press, 1909.

Leech, Margaret. *In the Days of McKinley.* New York: Harper and Brothers, 1959.

Leith, John H. *Creeds of the Churches.* Garden City, New York: Anchor Books, 1963.

Luebke, Frederick C. *Bonds of Loyalty.* DeKalb: Northern University Press, 1974.

----------. *Immigrants and Politics.* Lincoln, Nebraska: University of Nebraska Press, 1969.

MacLeish, Archibald, "American Letter: For Gerald Murphy." *The American Tradition in Literature,* 3rd ed., Sculley Bradley, Richmond Croom Beatty, and E. Hudson Long, eds. New York: W.W. Norton and Co., Inc., 1967.

Martin, William. *Switzerland from Roman Times to the Present.* Trans. Jocasta Innes. London: Elek Books Ltd., 1971.

Mayer, Kurt B. *The Population of Switzerland.* New York: Columbia University Press, 1952.

Morison, Samuel Eliot, Henry Steele Commager, and William E. Leuchtenburg. *The Growth of the American Republic.* New York: Oxford University Press, 1969.

Morison, Samuel Eliot. *The Oxford History of the American People.* New York: Oxford University Press, 1965.

Olson, James C. *History of Nebraska.* Lincoln, Nebraska: University of Nebraska Press, 1955.

Pattison, E. Mansell. *The Experience of Dying.* Englewood Cliffs, New Jersey: Prentice-Hall, Inc., 1977.

Peterson, H.C. *Propaganda for War.* Norman: University of Oklahoma Press, 1939.

Rölvaag, Ole E. *Giants in the Earth.* New York: Harper & Row, Pub., 1927.

Rooted in Faith, 75th Anniversary Book of Peace United Church of Christ, Tilden, Nebraska, 1977.

Sandoz, Marie. *Old Jules.* Lincoln, Nebraska: University of Nebraska Press, 1962.

Schelbert, Leo, ed. *New Glarus 1845-1970.* Glarus: Kommissionsverlag Tschudi & Co., AG, 1970.

Shannon, Fred A. *The Farmer's Last Frontier.* New York: Rinehart and Co., Inc., 1945.

Sheldon, Addison Erwin. *History and Stories of Nebraska.* Lincoln, Nebraska: University Publishing Co., 1929.

----------. *Nebraska the Land and the People I.* Chicago: Lewis Publishing Co., 1931.

Skårdal, Dorothy Burton. *The Divided Heart.* Lincoln, Nebraska: University of Nebraska Press, 1974.

Songbook for the Evangelical Church for German Evangelical Synod of North America. St. Louis: Eden Publishing House, 1908.

Stephenson, George M. *A History of American Immigration.* Boston: Ginn and Co., 1926.

Stumpp, Karl. *The Emigration from Germany to Russia in the Years 1763 to 1862.* Lincoln, Nebraska: American Historical Society of Germans from Russia, 1973.

Thürer, Georg. *Free and Swiss.* Trans. R.P. Hiller and E. Long. London: Oswald Wolf, 1970.

Timmons, Bascom N. *Portrait of an American: Charles G. Dawes.* New York: Henry Holt and Co., 1953.

Von Grueningen, John Paul, ed. *The Swiss in the United States.* Madison, Wisconsin: Swiss-American Historical Society, 1940.

Webb, Walter Prescott. *The Great Plains.* Boston: Ginn and Co., 1931.

Weber, Max. *The Protestant Ethic and the Spirit of Capitalism.* Trans. Talcott Parsons. New York: Charles Scribner's Sons, 1948.

Weinberg, Daniela. *Peasant Wisdom.* Berkeley: University of California Press, 1975.

Welsch, Roger. *Shingling the Fog and Other Plains Lies.* Chicago: Swallow Press, Inc., 1972.

Wittke, Carl. *We Who Built America.* New York: Prentice-Hall, Inc., 1940.

Winther, Sophus Keith. *Mortgage Your Heart.* New York: Macmillan Co., 1937.

----------. *Take All to Nebraska.* Lincoln, Nebraska: University of Nebraska Press, 1976.

Newspapers and Periodicals

All newspapers listed below are in the Nebraska State Historical Society, Lincoln, Nebraska. All were published in Nebraska.

Lincoln Daily Star, 1911.
Neligh Advocate, 1896.
Neligh Leader. 1903-1920.
Norfolk Daily News, 1903-1910
Oakdale Sentinel, 1893-1920
Tilden Citizen, 1893-1925, 1955. (Many issues are missing from 1893-1920)

Others

Einwanders Freund, Cleveland, Ohio. February, 1938.

Engel, George L., M.D. "Grief and Grieving," *American Journal of Nursing,* 64 (September 1964), 93-98.

Public Documents

Published Materials

Hayes, F.A., et al. *Soil Survey of Antelope County, Nebraska.* Washington: U.S. Dept. of Agriculture, 1924.

United States Census Office. *Twelfth Census of the United States: 1900. Agriculture,* I

United States Census Office. *Twelfth Census of the United States: 1900. Population,* I, Nebraska. Antelope County microfilm.

Unpublished Materials

"The Description of a Journal to My Native Country – Switzerland, and Return in 1913." In the private collection of Jeff Kappeler, Fremont, Nebraska.

Ives, Mrs. Lucius. "A History of Tilden." On file in the Tilden Public Library, Tilden, Nebraska.

Minutes of the Evangelical Friedens Church – 1903-1920. On file at Peace United Church of Christ, Tilden, Nebraska.

Minutes of the Women's Guild of Evangelical Friedens Church – 1903-1920. On file at Peace United Church of Christ, Tilden, Nebraska.

Letter and Interviews

Information in a letter to the author from Klara Stucki, Niece of Louise Ritter, Ins. Switzerland, 4 April 1978.

Interview with Dr. Jack Cady, Veterinarian, Arlington, Nebraska, February 1979.

Interviews with Ernest Ritter, Son of Louise Ritter, Tilden, Nebraska, 19 December 1978 and January 1979.

Interview with Mrs. Olga Ritter, Daughter-in-law of Louise Ritter, Tilden, Nebraska, January 1979.